P-47
THUNDERBOLT
at war

P-47
THUNDERBOLT
at war

William N. Hess

LONDON
IAN ALLAN LTD

First published 1976

ISBN 0 7110 0705 5

Designed by Nicholas Lerwill

© William N. Hess, 1976

Published by Ian Allan Ltd, Shepperton, Surrey,
and printed in the United Kingdom by
Ian Allan Printing Ltd.

Dedicated to Ann, my wife, and to the
thousands of Thunderbolt pilots
and their faithful groundcrews
who made it all possible

Contents

Introduction

In the course of World War II many types of fighter aircraft were introduced into combat. None probably received a more dubious reception than did Republic's P-47 Thunderbolt. When it first arrived in England many fighter pilots just shook their heads and walked away. "It's too big and too heavy", was the most common remark.

However, its brilliant designer, Alexander Kartveli, its builders at Republic Aircraft and the men who trained on the P-47 initially such as the 56th Fighter Group which went to the European Theatre of Operations (ETO) and the 348th Fighter Group which went to the Pacific, knew its capability and were sure that it would be successful — and it was.

Before World War II ended the famed Thunderbolt, or 'Jug' as it was known in some circles, built up a record of accomplishment in aerial warfare that is

challenged by few other fighter aircraft. In Northern Europe it pioneered bomber escort, defeated the cream of the Luftwaffe and established air superiority over the Reich even before the arrival of its worthy sucessor, the P-51 Mustang.

As a ground strafer and dive bomber it was without a doubt among the best. It did tremendous work in France and Germany, destroying literally thousands of vehicles, tanks, railroad locomotives and rolling stock. Hundreds of German troops on the ground fell before its guns and a host of enemy-held strong points were laid level by its bombs.

The Thunderbolt pilots of the Mediterranean bombed and strafed in front of Allied Armies moving up the leg of Italy and kept the enemy pinned down in the mountains right up to the very end.

Pacific P-47s helped win air superiority in the Southwest Pacific and furnished ground support to the island-hopping ground force throughout the war.

Thunderbolts of the 7th Air Force in the Central Pacific carried the war to the Japanese home islands and as far north as Korea and west to China. The enemy had no haven safe from their guns and bombs.

The men of the Royal Air Force and the US Army Air Force kept the Japanese out of the skies over India, China and Burma. Their P-47 units escorted the cargo aircraft flying the Hump and supported the Allied armies' drives in Burma and China. There was no better dive bombing and strafing done in the China, Burma, India Theatre than that by the Thunderbolts.

To tell the full story of 'The Thunderbolt at War' would encompass many volumes. It has been my humble effort to attempt to record some of the highlights of the P-47s career in the various theatres of operations. Much of this is related in the words of the men who took part in these actions. A number of these narratives were taken from the official US Air Force records which were made the same day of the combat operation. Other narratives have been furnished by a number of former P-47 pilots who have delved deeply into their records and memories to record the events of those days so many years ago. I am particularly indebted to these men for their efforts and very kind cooperation: Talmadge L. Ambrose, Air Chief Marshal Sir Neil Cameron, Brig. B. B. Cassidy, Jr, (Ret.), A. L. Coombs, Glenn A. Dow, Major Thomas F. Ellis, (Ret.), Robert T. Forrest, Preston Germain, Doug Parsons, Dustin Schlueter, A. B. Skidmore, Zell Smith, Jr and George L. Sutcliffe. I am very indebted to the P-47 Pilots' Association and its *Jugletter* editor, Mr Kevin Brown, for letting me use items from that publication.

Mrs Gloria Atkinson and the staff of the Simpson Historical Archives at Maxwell Air Force Base did their usual terrific job of assisting me in locating the vital official documentation utilised in this book. Many members of the P-47 Pilots' Association dug into their albums and foot-lockers to come up with many of the photographs which are reproduced. Of course, there were my fellow historians who came through with a number of photos: Gene Stafford, Kenn C. Rust, David Weatherill, Steve Birdsall, Joseph Maita and Gary Fry. My film processor and printer, John Bardwell, worked hard and long to come up with suitable prints made from many of the contributed photographs. My deepest appreciation to all.

Houston, Texas   *William N. Hess*

High above the clouds is 'Tony' a P-47 of the Air Sea Rescue Service. Slung underneath one wing is a life raft packet and marker flare packet is beneath the aft fuselage.

Left: The man who made the Thunder. Alexander Kartveli, who designed the P-47, was the brain behind the mating of the R-2800 engine and the plane around it. Kartveli was the father of the entire Thunder series at Republic — Thunderbolt, Thunderjet, Thunderflash and Thunderchief.

Below: Predecessor of the P-47 was the Seversky P-35. This sleek little aircraft was ordered in quantity by the US Army Air Corps and won the Bendix Air Races in 1937 with an average speed of 258mph between Burbank, California and Cleveland, Ohio.

Thunderbolt Origins

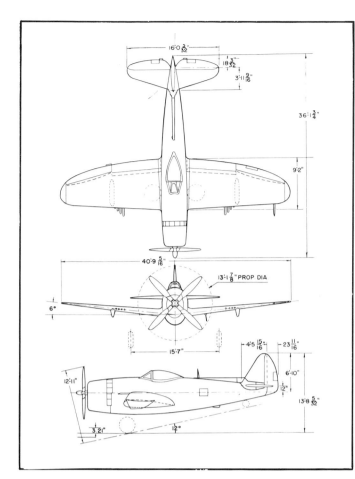

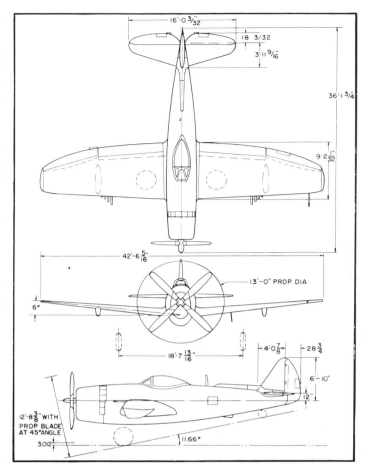

Above left: The XP-41 was built by Seversky in 1938 incorporated the Pratt and Whitney R-1830-19 engine and a two stage supercharger. Its performance was in excess of 300mph, but it was not ordered by the Air Corps.

Left: Skeleton view of a P-47-D-25 which incorporated the new bubble canopy. The ducting from the engine back to the turbo-supercharger aft of the pilot can be clearly seen in this drawing.

Above: Factory three view showing the vital dimensions of the P-47-D.

Above right: Factory three view showing the vital dimensions of the P-47-N.

Right: A Republic P-47-D-11-RE runs up its engine on the ramp at Republic aircraft. This version of the Thunderbolt was the first to employ water injection.

11

Test Flying the First Thunderbolt

The first flight of the XP-47-B was undertaken by Republic's chief test pilot, L. L. Brabham:

"The first flight was made May 6th, 1941, from the Republic airport at Farmingdale, Long Island, but, due to the condition of our unpaved runway, arrangements were made with the Army Air Corps to land at Mitchel Field a few miles away. As you may know, the XP-47 aircraft had a door on the left side for entry and exit, so the canopy couldn't be opened. The door was jettisonable for baleout, but in flight the only way to get large quantities of air into the cockpit was by opening a small side panel. On the first takeoff, the cockpit filled with smoke which had come from oil spilling on the exhaust pipe running just beneath the cockpit to the turbo-supercharger. And, because the airflow over the windshield caused a low pressure in the cockpit, when I opened the panel it just pulled in that much more smoke and it was almost impossible to breathe. But, since my boss had expressed a wish to see the first takeoff at Farmingdale, and also to see the first landing at Mitchel — and liking my job and remembering my Air Corps' training that the boss's wish was the boss's command — I just held my breath most of the time to give him and the other VIPs time to drive from Farmingdale to Mitchel.

"Otherwise, there was very little wrong with the airplane when I landed at Mitchel. Flutter analysis showed some suspicious trends within the operating speed of the aircraft, so it was decided to make the necessary alterations to the wing at Mitchel, prior to further flight test. The wing-structure modifications required only about two pounds of stiffeners per wing to change the vibration frequency to a speed well above the operating range of the P-47. There were some other things, like control forces and response, which had to be improved, but the solutions were well known and easily incorporated. It was obvious to me, from the first few minutes of flight that we had a superior airplane, one that just had to be a winner. So, after the work was completed at Mitchel, we got right into the engineering evaluation.

"Since this was the first operational combat airplane with a turbo-supercharger, and a potential 40 000 foot ceiling, the high altitude work became the most interesting portion of the flght tests. First problem to be encountered was ignition breakdown, due to arcing in the low density above 30 000 feet. It was finally solved by a vast amount of research in ignition systems, and by pressurising the ignition harness. Next problem was oil cavitation. With the lowered boiling point above 30 000 feet, the oil was boiling off, and the resulting foam couldn't be forced through the bearings.

"After the usual procedure of performance, stability and control, and power plant tests, we went into the spin and dive tests. I did the initial spin tests, with a minimum entering altitude of 20 000 feet, and followed with the dive tests, reaching an indicated air speed of 550 mph and a mach number of .80. The final dive proved the fabric tail used on the early aircraft to be unsafe, so we changed to all metal control surfaces."

Into Combat

Left: Lineup of P-47-Cs belonging to the 63rd Fighter Squadron, 56th Fighter Group. The 56th was the original Thunderbolt unit to arrive in England.

Below: P-47C-2-RE of the 4th Fighter Group's 335th Squadron. The white stripes on the tail and white nose band were for quick recognition. Additionally, the blue circle of the national insignia is banded in yellow.

The first P-47-Cs began to arrive in England during December 1942 and assembly of the aircraft was begun immediately. As soon as one was made airworthy it was sent to the testing facility at Bovingdon for performance evaluation under the direction of Colonel Cass Hough, test pilot and engineer for the US 8th Air Force.

Colonel Hough put the Thunderbolt through its paces in an intensive two week programme which was climaxed by matching the aircraft against a captured Focke Wulf 190A. At altitudes below 15 000 feet the Focke Wulf out-turned and out-ran the heavy American fighter at will. The only appreciable manoeuverability possessed by the P-47 at low altitudes was at an airspeed in excess of 250 miles per hour.

However, at altitudes above 15 000 feet combat with the Focke Wulf was another story. At these altitudes the Thunderbolt was not only faster than its German opponent, but it also out-turned it. Although the Focke Wulf could pull away from the P-47 in a dive at first, the Thunderbolt quickly built up speed and closed the gap.

Of course, there was no way the P-47 could be restricted from operations below 15 000 feet and its early missions would primarily consist of fighter sweeps over the enemy coast. So it was not without misgivings that the P-47s were assigned to the 8th Air Force.

The first Thunderbolts were assigned to three fighter groups. These units were the 4th Fighter Group at Debden in Essex, the 78th Fighter Group at Goxhill in North Lincolnshire and the 56th Fighter Group at Kings Cliffe in Norfolk. The veteran fighter pilots who had flown Spitfires with the Royal Air Force and who composed the nucleus of the 4th Group were appalled when they saw their first P-47s. After months of flying the slim

Below: Thunderbolts of the 335th Fighter Squadron, 4th Fighter Group forming up over England in 1943. The former Spitfire pilots of the 4th Group just couldn't believe that the P-47 was a fighter plane.

Bottom: Two P-47-C's of the 61st Fighter Squadron line up for take off on the grass at Horsham St. Faith.

and sleek Spitfires they just couldn't believe that the massive monster with the big radial engine could even be called a fighter. Even after months of successful combat in the P-47, the men of the 4th Group never really adjusted to it.

The 78th Group had come to England flying P-38s, only to have them taken away for the North African campaign. Along with the aircraft went most of the junior pilots. The leaders left had to set up a training schedule with new pilots and start in from scratch with the Thunderbolt. However, most were just elated to get new aircraft to fly.

The 56th Group had trained in the P-47 and were eager to make their combat debut. Before this was possible all three groups had to undergo training flights and maintenance men had to make modifications before the Thunderbolt was ready for its first combat mission.

On April 8th, 1943, a combined force made up of 24 P-47s from all three operational groups participated in an uneventful fighter sweep over the Straits of Dover. Several other missions were mounted before first contact was made with the enemy and the Thunderbolt scored its first victory.

This took place on April 15th, 1943, and the victor was a veteran Eagle Squadron pilot, Major Donald J. M. Blakeslee. "I left Felixstowe at 1701 hours on course," related Blakeslee, "when I discovered that my gyro was unserviceable. Continuing by compass, I first saw the enemy coast near Knocke (Belgium) about 20 miles north of my intended landfall, flying at 29 000 feet.

"I saw five vapor trails headed west about five miles north of Knocke and 5 000 feet below over the water. I made a turn to port and saw three FW 190s below, flying southwest. As soon as they saw us, they turned inland and started home. Selecting the nearest one, who was in a 15° or 20° dive, I started down after him. Two unidentified P-47s took a short burst at him at long range and broke away right and left. I trimmed my kite for a steep dive and found myself overtaking him rapidly. His only evasive action was to increase his dive. I opened fire at about 700 yards, closing to 500 yards still firing. I saw tracers going over his canopy, so I increased the angle of my dive and sawed through him twice. I saw many hits behind, in and in front of his cockpit. He lurched sharply and a fraction of a second later crashed into the ground, exploding.

"My entire attack was made from directly astern and slightly above. I pulled out of my dive below 500 feet and found myself approaching Ostend. I went over the centre of the city at about 300 feet and was not fired on. Proceeding to about mid Channel on the deck, I climbed to about 3 000 feet and returned to base, landing at 1820. My number two was engaged when he was attempting to follow me down and I returned alone."

The men of the 4th Group destroyed two more enemy aircraft on the mission, but the mixed force of 59 Thunderbolts lost three of their own. When congratulated for his demonstration that a P-47 could out-dive the Focke Wulf, Blakeslee retorted "By God, it ought to dive. It certainly won't climb."

Regardless, the early combat tactics of the Thunderbolt had been demonstrated. Whenever the P-47 pilot was able to utilise the diving speed of the aircraft and the concentrated firepower of the eight 50 calibre machine guns in the wings, there was no escape for the enemy.

Flying practice formation over the English countryside are P-47-Cs of the 62nd Squadron of the 56th Group. Note the individual call letter of each aircraft painted aft of the national insignia.

Escort Fighter

Resplendent in their olive drab paint are these P-47s of the 56th Fighter Group forming up over England. Many of the crew chiefs waxed their charges to give them a bit more speed.

At first the use of the P-47 as an escort fighter had one great drawback. The big R-2800 Pratt and Whitney engine drank fuel so rapidly that it severely limited the range of the aircraft. Upon the arrival of the P-47s in England, pressurised auxiliary fuel tanks for use at high altitude had not been perfected and once this problem was overcome, the tanks were just not available in sufficient quantity.

The 75-gallon metal tanks gave the P-47 a range of 280 miles but these were not put into use until August 1943. The 108-gallon paper tanks which were manufactured and perfected in England didn't put in their combat appearance until September 1943. However, the latter tank gave the Thunderbolt a range of 325 miles and put the aircraft in the long-range escort business.

The first bomber escort mission was undertaken on May 14th 1943, when 118 Thunderbolts set out to take the B-17s to Antwerp, Belgium. Even without drop tanks the P-47s could handle assignments in this range. A number of Messerschmitt 109s and Focke Wulf 190s opposed the escort and a heated air battle took place. Using their proven diving attack tactics the P-47 pilots accounted for four of the enemy but lost three of their own, including Colonel Arman Peterson, Commander of the 78th Group.

The next escort mission did not take place until June 12th 1943, with Colonel Hubert 'Hub' Zemke, Commander of the 56th Group leading. "As flying wing commander of the 56th Fighter Group on this mission," Zemke reported, "I had decided that I would lead the 61st Fighter Squadron as 'bouncing' squadron. The 62nd Fighter Squadron was to be close escort at the same altitude and slightly to the rear. The 63rd Fighter Squadron was to be high cover for the other two squadrons with a superiority of one to two thousand feet more or less to the inside of the course and slightly ahead where I could direct their direction and disposition.

"Take off and climb of the squadrons was normal. The squadrons positioned themselves on the climb so that the 63rd was on the left and the 62nd was on the right. From Felixstowe to Gravelines the course was 174 degrees thru' a thin layer of about 6/10 cirrus cloud. This gave me considerable anxiety as the 56th Group was to give high support to the 4th Fighter Group. The layer being at 26 000 feet. At this same time, which was about 0930 plus hours, contrails were reported ahead going into France and were believed to be the 4th Fighter Group. Shortly thereafter, ground operations reported bandits in the vicinity of Ostend heading west along the coast. Since the group had not reached France and were trying to give support to the 4th Fighter Group, who were only in visual contact by their occasional condensation trails ahead, it was decided to continue on plan.

"At about 0935 hours, while still over water, ground operations reported that 20 plus bandits were in the Lille area, heading northwest (in our direction) altitude unknown.

"When the coast was reached at 0937 hours, a slight turn left was made placing the 63rd slightly ahead and well to the left, they having gained two thousand feet of altitude over the remainder of the group. Again ground operations gave us instructions that 20 plus bandits were flying northwest at 20 000 feet in the vicinity of Ypres, this being due ahead of us on course.

"A split second later I looked ahead at 11 o'clock and down slightly toward a very large hole in the cirrus cloud and saw fifteen or twenty spots climbing in our direction. Some of these spots were leaving distinct vapor trails. They must have been 15 or 20 miles away at the time. They, as well as we, never altered our course but closed at a very rapid rate.

"When a distance of two or three miles between forces had been reached, I saw that they were flying in three groups of approximately six each in what would be called a 'company-front' formation. They were then below some three or four thousand feet and well to my left. The altitude of my squadron was 27 000 feet at that time.

"The squadrons were told that I was taking the first section of eight of the 61st Fighter Squadron in a left diving attack. It may be noted that I forgot to touch my throttle and it remained at 31 inches manifold pressure and 2550rpm for the entire combat.

"At first I dove to attack the lower lead unit, but changed my mind and continued down to attack a group who were slightly to the rear and above the lead unit. As the attacking dive commenced, the lead enemy aircraft (e/a) group began turning to the right and the remainder did likewise. This fact plus the fact that they never flew more than two or three airplane lengths apart, leads me to believe that I was never seen but that all eyes were on the 63rd Fighter Squadron which was well to my left and directly over the hole in the overcast.

"As I approached the last of the four enemy aircraft, directly astern, I noticed

One of the greatest fighter group leaders in the 8th Air Force was Colonel Hubert 'Hub' Zemke of the 56th Group. The inscription written in Russian on the aircraft means "My Comrade".

that the tail end aircraft had white stripes around the horizontal stabilizer and elevators. This made me hesitate for I thought these aircraft might have been P-47s coming out of France. Perhaps this hesitation helped me, for I closed to 150 to 200 yards before firing. There was no doubt in my mind then. To destroy this aircraft was a mere matter of putting the dot on the fuselage and pulling the trigger. A split second after firing, the fuselage burst into flames and pieces of the right wing came off. It immediately went down to the right leaving the number three plane of the four aircraft string just ahead.

"This plane for some reason must have been weaving so that I had to give it some deflection. The deflection proved to be a bit excessive and I noticed strikes out on the right wing tip. The plane being in a right bank went down placing me directly in back of the number two plane of the string, which sat in the gun sight as one would imagine for the ideal shot. Again, when the trigger was pulled this aircraft exploded with a long sheet of flame and smoke.

"Unfortunately, the number one man of the flight of FW 190s must have become aware of the unhealthy situation and left the scene of battle in a dive so I didn't see him go.

"Each gun fired an average of 50 rounds in the three bursts mentioned above.

"Recovery was made ahead at 26 000 feet where a slight turn to the left was made and I then found Dunkirk directly down to my left.

"On looking over the sky again, everything was well broken up and miles away. Only two other P-47s were with me out of the sixteen taken out. Combats were noted at great distances away so I ordered an assembly over Dunkirk. This was exceedingly difficult as the R/T was nearly jammed with pilots reporting each other and e/a as can be imagined.

"The assembly point was moved out over the sea from Dunkirk as heavy anti-aircraft was put up over the area. The squadrons were then ordered home, since the e/a had gone to the deck and it was believed all organisations were disorganised. In reality the 62nd and 63rd Fighter Squadrons never entered the battle. I had failed to call them down until too late. The group continued on to home base with the two above mentioned squadrons giving support and picking up my stragglers."

Heated air battles would continue to take place for many months to come as the Thunderbolts challenged the

Luftwaffe for supremacy of the air over and along the bomber streams. Whereas the daylight bomber offensive had been facing only 350 German fighters in the West in January 1943, by June some 600 Luftwaffe elite fighters from Jagdeschwader 1, 2 and 26 were in position.

July 28th, 1943 was a milestone in the escort career of the Thunderbolt for on that day jettisonable belly tanks were carried for the first time. This enabled them to act as withdrawal escort for B-17s returning from targets in Northwest Germany. The 4th Fighter Group carried the tanks and apparently surprised the Luftwaffe as they ganged up on the crippled Fortresses on their way home. Some 45 of the enemy were encountered and nine of them fell while only one friendly fighter was lost. The Thunderbolt had won its spurs as an escort fighter.

Top: Typical foggy English morning sees the crew chief of 'PZ-K' getting his P-47 ready for one of the early escort missions. Slung below the belly of this 386th Fighter Squadron craft is a 75 gallon 'tear-drop' auxiliary tank which boosted P-47 range to 240 miles.

Above: A most welcome sight to the harried gunners on the heavy bombers of the 8th Air Force were P-47s cavorting off their wings. However, woe be to the fighter pilot that turned his nose in towards one of the 'Big Friends'.

Taking It

A damaged Thunderbolt of the
56th Fighter Group.

On June 26, 1943 the 56th Fighter Group was assigned the task of providing the B-17s' withdrawal support from an aircraft factory target in the Paris area. Forty-nine Thunderbolts took off from Horsham St Faith, Norfolk, the new base of the Zemke-led unit, stopped at Manston in Kent to top their fuel tanks, and were on their way to the rendezvous. They had just met the Fortresses in the vicinity of Forges, France, when 40 to 60 FW 190s and Me 109s put in an appearance. The men of the 56th turned into the enemy immediately and were successful in breaking up the attacking formations. However, the P-47s lost four of their number and had several aircraft so badly damaged that they were unfit for further service. Lt Gerald W. Johnson was credited with the only American victory of the day.

Those who may have had doubts about the ability of the P-47 to take punishment and still fly had only to talk to Lt Robert S. Johnson after his return. Had it not been for the miraculous escape by Johnson that day, which was due entirely to the tough P-47, he would never have made it back to England to become the first American fighter ace to break the World War I record of Captain Eddie Rickenbacker with a grand total of 28 aerial victories.

Here in Bob Johnson's own words is what happened:

"My position was Shaker Yellow number four. We were entering France, just north of Dieppe, climbing at 180mph at 27 000 feet, when I spotted 16 FW 190s turning in directly behind us. They were in line abreast and came from over the water by the same path we did. I called them in when they were still some distance from us. They were about 1 000 feet below us, apparently coming out of a dive and had much more speed than we did. We stayed line abreast for a second or so longer. Then I heard a rattling and some thudding on my plane. My plane was thrown down to the right and my engine quit, or rather, sounded like I have blown a cylinder head. Flame and smoke filled my cockpit and I tried to open the canopy. I could only get it open about nine inches so I stood on the dash board and heaved but it still wouldn't open. I yelled 'May Day' several times and then worked on the canopy again. All but a few small pieces of the glass then disappeared. I began to think about what I

Lt Robert S. Johnson's Thunderbolt on return to base on June 26th, 1943, after taking all the firepower the enemy could bring to bear.

was going to do. I was turning toward the coast and had about 19 000 feet of altitude (while coming down I had dived through the Fortresses). I saw several FW 190s, swung in their direction and fired a burst at them. I could not see ahead since my windshield was more like a blind flying hood, being covered with oil. I decided that if I went down near the coast of France, I would certainly be captured so I turned back inland and was going to go as far inland and southwards as possible before leaving the plane. It was then that I throttled back and found that my engine would run at low speeds. I began to think that I might be able to get the plane far enough into the Channel to be picked up by the British.

"I turned around and glided towards the north. I was about seven or eight thousand feet about ten miles south of Dieppe and about the same distance inland when a single FW 190 jumped me. The FW 190 was colored a deep sky blue and had a yellow nose. When I first saw him he was coming in at my level from four o'clock. I flew straight ahead wondering what he was going to do. I supposed he was going to watch me go in the drink, so I just kept going slightly downwards. He came up to within fifty yards and still did not fire but I was afraid he was going to close completely up to me and fire, so I kicked it around into him. He pulled up, got on my tail and peppered away. I wanted to get to England or as close as possible, so I applied right and then left rudder alternately and kept heading north. He came past me, going much faster than I was, and I fired in his direction. I was only gliding at 180 miles per hour. He came up along side of me and flew for several minutes. I waved and he returned the wave, then he pulled up, fired another short burst and then left me.

"I was about 4 000 feet about five miles northwest of Dieppe at that time. I zoom climbed up to 8 000 feet and called 'May Day'. The distance to England was more than I had imagined, so I called for a homing. They brought me to the south coast of England. The hydraulic fluid was a half inch thick on the floor of my cockpit and it kept flying up into my eyes, so I flew with eyes closed half of the time. I landed at Manston. I had no brakes or flaps, couldn't see ahead, and had my wheels down, so I ground looped to stop the plane."

No wonder the German pilot shook his head as the P-47 flown by Lt Bob Johnson continued on towards England. A very lucky Thunderbolt pilot, Bob Johnson went on to become a top-scoring 28-victory ace in the 56th Group.

Big Day at Duxford

The 78th Fighter Group had moved to Duxford on April 1st, 1943 and it was from this base that they began their combat operations. The 78th had been in the thick of things from the beginning and had scored a number of early victories

The mission of July 30th, 1943, would prove to be a real milestone in the combat history of the 78th. That day the group carried drop tanks for the first time which enabled them to venture a few miles into Germany proper. The Luftwaffe came up in force to meet the bombers and the men of the 78th roared down to the attack. When combat was broken off the Thunderbolt pilots from Duxford had become the first American unit to run its victories into two figures; seven Me 109s and nine FW 190s. Captain Charles London became the first fighter ace of the

Left: Captain Charles P. London became the first ace of the 8th Air Force on June 30th, 1943, when he downed a Messerschmitt 109 and a Focke Wulf 190 for his fourth and fifth victories.

Below: The hardworking and faithful ground crews of the 78th Fighter Group loading new 108 gallon paper tanks that increased range to 325 miles. Had the AAF made earlier strides in the development of drop tanks, deeper escort for the hard-pressed bombers would have been possible sooner.

First P-47 pilot to score a triple victory over Europe was Major Eugene Roberts of the 78th Fighter Group. He is shown here indicating the two subsequent victories that made him an ace.

8th Air Force when he downed two enemy aircraft and Major Eugene P. Roberts became the first fighter pilot of the 8th Air Force to score a triple victory on one mission. Lt Quince Brown became the first American pilot to strafe ground targets when he shot up a locomotive and a gun emplacement. However, the mission was not without tragedy. Among the three pilots lost by the group that day was Lt Col Melvin McNickle, the Commander of the 78th.

The events of that historic day for the men from Duxford are related by Major Eugene P. Roberts:

"I was flying as Group Leader on bomber withdrawal support mission on 30th July 1943. We took off with belly tanks, climbed to 23 000 feet over the Channel. Dropped tanks about 15 miles off coast of Holland. Southeast of Noordwal we crossed coast at 27 000 feet, indicating 180mph. Our course took us just north of Hellevotsluis over Dordrecht to the south of Nijmegen and just south of Haldern — the rendezvous point. We continued almost to Raesfeld. When we sighted the bombers off to our left we made a 90 degree turn and picked up bombers, approximately over Winterswijk. One straggling bomber was observed, flying below the main formation in a dive, trailing black smoke and being attacked by about five enemy aircraft. I peeled my flight down and to the rear of the straggler. This would be about 1 000 feet below the main formation of bombers and would be at about 21 000 feet. All e/a sighted us and took evasive action to the extent that I was unable to close, although I did fire a burst with improper deflection. The e/a was in a diving attack from the rear on this straggler. I initiated my attack from the port side rear of the fighters, swinging in behind them in their dive. They rolled to the left, then pulled up in a climbing turn to the right and broke sharply downward to the rear. I followed one of them in the climb, attempting to get a deflection shot. When he broke downward, I found I was directly beneath the bombers and saw a number of ball turret gunners firing at my flight. I broke down and to the rear, and pulled up to starboard side of bombers about 1 000 yards out and at about their level. Looking up, I observed six e/a flying parallel to the bombers, and about 1 000 feet directly above me. They failed to see us and did not take any action, so after they passed I made a climbing turn to the left to come up to their level and behind them. At this point I missed my second element, and

found myself alone with my wingman. In our pull up we missed the original six e/a sighted, but sighted a single e/a ahead on same level at about 1 500 yards. I dived slightly below, opened full throttle and closed to about 400 yards. I pulled up directly behind e/a and opened fire. Several strikes were observed on e/a, his wheels dropped and he spun down, trailing large volume of dark smoke and flame.

"I continued parallel to the bombers and sighted two more e/a about 2 000 yards ahead. I used the same tactics, closing to 400 yards astern, pulled up and opened fire on port aircraft. Observed several strikes and e/a billowed smoke and flame, rolled over and went down. I was closing so fast that I had to pull up to avoid hitting him.

"I observed my wingman, F/O Koontz, firing at the second, or starboard aircraft, but did not see the results, as he was under me. Both these aircraft were FW 190s. After this second engagement, we were about two miles ahead of the bombers, so I cut across, falling in behind him. We started to close again, using the same tactics as in the two previous attacks to get within range. This e/a, a Me 109, peeled to starboard to attack bombers ahead-on, and I followed, closing to 500 yards before opening fire. Two bursts were behind, but the third caught him and he spun down, trailing smoke and flame, some 1 500 yards ahead of the bombers.

"I found myself on the same level as the bombers and approaching them head-on with no alternative other than to fly between their two main formations. They did not fire on me. This action took place about the vicinity of Rhenon, Holland. After flying through the bombers, I pulled to the left out on their starboard side, flying parallel and on their level, heading home. I then observed two e/a attacking a P-47 ahead and above me. They were flying 180 degrees to me so I could not close effectively to help, but did fire a burst at the leading aircraft with not enough deflection to be effective. The P-47 dove and passed under me, taking evasive action in his dive; I did not see him again. I headed out and joined another element led by Captain Irvin and proceeded home out over Overflakkee Island at 23 000 feet, indicating 230mph.

"In the area we were engaged, there must have been 80 to 100 single engine enemy fighters manoeuvering for attacks. I feel that our efforts prevented 80% of these e/a from attacking while we were in the vicinity."

Escort in Relays

Two yellow and black
checkered nosed P-47-D s of the
351st Fighter Squadron, 353rd
Fighter Group pull in close to
one of the "Big Friends".
Mixed formations of olive drab
and natural metal finished
aircraft became common by
mid-1944.

By the fall of 1943, Eighth Fighter Command boasted a total of six Thunderbolt groups. The 352nd, 353rd and 355th Groups had arrived and by early September all were in action. These reinforcements boosted the total of fighters available for escort to approximately 240 Thunderbolts and made possible bomber escort in relays. One force would be dispatched to rendezvous with the bombers at a given point to provide escort for the first phase of penetration, a second force would provide escort for another phase of penetration, a third force would be utilised as target area escort and further groups of fighters would protect the bombers on their withdrawal.

To defend their targets the Luftwaffe continued to build up forces of interceptors, including large numbers of twin-engined Messerschmitt 110 and 210s plus Junkers Ju 88s, all equipped with rockets. These projectiles could be fired into the bomber formations while the enemy aircraft were still beyond the machine-gun range of the gunners on the bombers. To bring the twin-engined fighters into the fight while escort was still present was a complete fiasco as was proven on a mission of October 8th, 1943, when the bomber force was dispatched to bomb Bremen.

The Luftwaffe was fully alerted for the raid and were positioned to attack just as soon as the American force crossed the Dutch coast. Not only were the Messerschmitt 109s and Focke Wulf 190s orbiting in wait, but the twin-engined Messerschmitt 110s were there, too. What the Thunderbolts of the 56th Group did to the Messerschmitt 110s is related by P-47 ace, Lt Colonel F. S. Gabreski:

"My squadron positioned itself on the left flank of the bombers and no enemy aircraft were encountered until we were about to break off our escort in the vicinity of Hanover. As we were making our last run along the flank of the bombers, Lt Foster, Red One, called in a formation about 7 o'clock to us at 12 000 feet. He suggested that I take a 180 degree turn to the left and I would be in a perfect position for a bounce. No sooner said than done. A 180 degree turn was completed and that put us directly up sun and White flight dove down from 22 000 feet in a

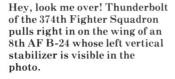

Hey, look me over! Thunderbolt of the 374th Fighter Squadron pulls right in on the wing of an 8th AF B-24 whose left vertical stabilizer is visible in the photo.

perfectly coordinated attack which put the three flights directly astern of each other, well spaced to the rear. The Me 110s flew in two sections astern. About six to seven planes in the first section, echeloned to the right and about the same in the second section, also echeloned to the right. The distance between sections was about 700 yards. A perfect set up.

"I dove through the first section, opened fire at 800 yards, picking the second man from the extreme right. I closed to about 50 yards. The Me 110 lost his tail and wing in the attack, while I proceeded to continue my pass towards the first section of Me 110s. I again opened fire at about 500 yards and saw strikes all over the fuselage and wing of the ship flying on the extreme right. I closed to about 50 feet and broke off. The enemy aircraft exploded and pieces hit the ground.

"By the time that I regained a little altitude and completed a turn, it appeared to me that the enemy planes in both sections were destroyed with the exception of one. The sky was still littered with burning planes and chutes floating through the sky. Actually, there were six to seven chutes seen in the vicinity. It must have been the most perfect show that I have ever been on. In my estimation the pilots that flew with me were perhaps the best that I ever had the pleasure of flying with. It seems that nothing escapes them. Before we had time to actually get together again, I spotted the lone Me 110 that had gotten away. I dove from 12 000 feet to 5 000 feet before I closed to about 1 800 yards. At this moment, the Me 110 started diving away down into the clouds. I closed to about 900 yards and fired just before the plane hit the overcast. A few hits were observed around the wing roots, and just as I was about to close in for a good shot, the German hit the cloud. I broke up and regained about 14 000 feet of my altitude and proceeded towards home. Much to my surprise, the entire squadron was still pretty much intact. Six planes returned as a flight while six more proceeded just a little ahead and above. A more perfect exhibition has never been displayed at any show by a squadron of men who are really eager to destroy the enemy."

Two ground crewmen of the 56th Group remove a 108 gallon tank from the stack to carry it over to be fitted on an aircraft. These tanks of compressed paper were made in England on an emergency basis.

Striking High and Low

Right: Standard mounting of a 500 pound bomb underneath the wing of a P-47. These wing pylons were factory installed beginning with the P-47D-15-RE models.

Below: This 353rd Group Thunderbolt is really 'loaded for bear'. A 500 pound bomb is slung under each wing along with cluster tubes for 4.5 inch rockets. Slung underneath the belly is a 150 gallon fuel tank.

November 1943 saw the P-47 Thunderbolt initiate a new type of mission that in time would gain it undying fame. Colonel 'Hub' Zemke of the 56th Fighter Group decided that the time had come to go after the Luftwaffe on its own airfields. He persuaded 8th Bomber Command to lend him a B-24 bomber to act as lead aircraft in his plan. The multi-engined aircraft with a bombardier in the nose would zero in on the target through his bomb sight and the fighter pilots would release their 500-pound bombs on his signal.

While Zemke was working on level bombing for his P-47s, Lt Col Loren G. McCollom set his 353rd Fighter Group to work on dive bombing. Through trial and error the Thunderbolt pilots found that best results were obtained by pushing over into their dives from 18 000 to 20 000 feet, taking a downward run of some 5 000 feet and releasing the bomb. Once the bomb was gone the Thunderbolt pilot effected a high speed pull out and departed the area.

Both groups put their respective plans

into operation on November 25th, 1943. Lt Colonel David Schilling led the Thunderbolts of the 56th accompanied by their B-24. The 62nd Squadron echeloned to the rear and right of the bomber while the 61st Squadron was to the left. The 63rd Squadron flew directly astern and to the left rear of the bomber. Unfortunately, the bomb release system on the B-24 malfunctioned and all bombs dropped late. What might have been a satisfactory strike on the airfield St Omer/Longunesse resulted in only slight damage.

The same day 16 Thunderbolts were airborne enroute to drop 500-pound bombs on the airfield St. Omer/Ft Rouge. Escort for the bomb carrying aircraft was provided by the balance of the 353rd Fighter Group and some aircraft from the 78th Group.

The plan called for the dive bombing craft to attack in flights of four, with each flight dropping on signal from the flight leader. On arrival over the target area heavy flak was encountered. Just as Colonel McCollom committed his flight

Another great leader and outstanding fighter tactician of the 56th Fighter Group was Lt Col Dave Schilling. Schilling took over the group in the summer of 1944 after Zemke went to take over another group.

to their bomb run his P-47 was hit by flak, burst into flames and the pilot baled out to become a prisoner of war.

Although the bombing experiment had not proved to be greatly successful, it set a pattern for later operations which would establish the Thunderbolt as one of the greatest fighter-bomber aircraft of the war.

The following day a record number of Thunderbolts were airborne in relays to provide escort for the bomber stream on a mission to Bremen. As the bombers rallied off the target they were set upon by swarms of enemy fighters, including some 50-60 twin-engined types. These German aircraft were closing rapidly on the bomber stream from directly astern when the Thunderbolts of the 56th Fighter Group appeared.

"I was leading Postgate Blue Flight," related Captain Walker M. Mahurin, "and flying at about 27 000 feet when we first (about 1207 hours) sighted the 'Big Friends' south of Oldenburg on the same level and off to our left. The squadron started a left turn to take position on the left side of the bombers, when I first sighted enemy aircraft. At the rear about five miles and slightly above I saw about eight single engined craft making condensation trails. I called them in but, since they were not attacking my attention turned to the many trails at the rear of the bomber formation and on the same level. These I decided to bounce.

"I cut back the throttle and started down on one Me 110 that was flying on the same course as the bombers, slightly behind and on the same level. I closed on the e/a but I believe that he saw us because he broke left and headed straight down. At this time my wingman and my second element broke away from me and attacked this e/a. I did not see the result of this attack because I started on another e/a.

"The second Me 110 was flying in the same direction as the first, but it was close enough to be lobbing rockets into the Fortress formation. As I approached from directly astern I saw several flashes

Nose-on view of P-47-D loaded with a 500 pound bomb under each wing and sporting black and white invasion stripes. These stripes were hurriedly applied on the night of June 5th, 1944, to all Allied aircraft that were to fly over the invasion fleet the next day.

from rockets in and around the bombers. As I opened fire at about four hundred yards, there were many flashes all around the Me 110. One or more of his rockets exploded, and many large pieces blew off of the ship. The e/a flipped over to the right and I went by within twenty yards of it. At the time the canopy was completely off of the ship and the rear gunner was half in and half out of the ship dangling in the breeze. I watched the e/a head for the ground with flames coming from the right engine. A large object fell from the plane and later a parachute opened. I claim this Me 110 destroyed.

"As I broke right from this attack I saw another attack going in on the rear of the bomber formation. Under almost the same circumstances I again made an attack. This time the Me 110 was firing at the lower Fortress and he was well within range of the Fortress because as I opened fire I saw tracers leave the Fortress and pass by the canopy of my ship. When I fired I noticed numerous hits all over the Me 110. It too fell off to the left and, as I passed by it, the right engine was a mass of flame extending the length of the ship. It was spinning down. I again broke right and started to climb. I claim this Me 110 destroyed.

"As I circled again I noticed another Me 110 in the same position as the rest. I opened my throttle and started to chase him. As I closed in on him I saw him start to fire at the Forts. When I fired at him I saw many hits about the wings and fuselage and the ship went from straight level to a vertical position as if the pilot had suddenly pushed forward on the stick

A 1 000 pound bomb loaded underneath the belly of a Thunderbolt. Pull out after dropping this projectile required 1 500 feet to avoid the blast.

A real lethal load to be used against ground targets when the 8th AF went down to earth was a combination of a 250 pound bomb and clusters of fragmentation bombs.

A rather unusual armament combination of two 250 pound bombs and a 75 gallon metal drop tank.

with all his might. As I watched it go down, I did not see any flames, but the ship was heading straight for the deck. I claim this Me 110 as a probable.

"I again made another circle and sighted a Me 110 off the right of the bombers and slightly below. I had my throttle wide open at the time and I began to chase him. Just as I came to within about four hundred yards of the e/a three Thunderbolts passed by me and began to fire at the e/a. I later found out that it was led by Lt Bryant of the 62nd Squadron. The whole flight was firing and Lt Bryant was in such a position that the smoke from his guns passed over my ship. The e/a was devastated. I fired a short burst, but make no claim.

"When I pulled up this time, I passed a Me 109 going in the opposite direction on the same level as I was. The e/a started to come around behind me, but just then a flight of Thunderbolts came into view and the Me 109 started to turn with them. I got up sun on it and when it came by I started down on it. The e/a flipped over on its back and when I last saw it, it was headed straight down. I did not fire and make no claims.

"At this time (1229 hours) the Group Commander announced over the radio that the Group should leave the bombers. I found myself on the right side slightly below the bombers headed out. At this time I saw another Me 110 headed for the deck, flying in the same direction as the 'Big Friends'. I called to two Thunderbolts several thousand feet above me to watch my tail and I started to attack. I followed the e/a down to fourteen thousand feet where I caught it. When I opened fire from about four hundred yards I saw my tracers leave my ship and hit the e/a directly in the fuselage. As I closed on the e/a I saw hits all over both engines and the fuselage. As I passed the e/a it was flaming fiercely in both engines and fuselage. I claim this Me 110 destroyed.

"Again I opened the throttle and climbed back to 26 000 feet. I was picked up by two men from another squadron and escorted home.

"My engagements lasted from the time my squadron hit the bombers (about 1207 hours) until several minutes after the Group Commander notified us to leave (1231 hours). During that time I would estimate I had full boost for at least thirty minutes. Although my engine was overheated and running rough I was able to make the trip home uneventfully.

"In regard to tactics, I think that it was important to note that the twin engined e/a had adopted a formation which resembled the one flown by the Fortresses. They were to the rear of the Fortress formation but they appeared from above to be a group of our bombers that was straggling. Only when I was close enough to positively identify them was I able to ascertain that they were e/a. They were painted a color similar to the color of our bombers. All of the aircraft that I saw appeared to have rockets mounted outboard of both engines and in between the engines and fuselage. Outside the first one, none of them took any evasive action whatsoever, and I believe that they did not expect us."

The Thunderbolts of 8th Fighter Command were credited with downing 36 enemy aircraft that day with the 56th Group establishing a new record by chalking up 26 of the victories.

P-47D-30-RE of the 56th Fighter Group undergoing gun-calibration. The .50 calibres were harmonised with the gun sight for converging fire at 150-300 yards depending on the personal preference of the individual pilot.

Blocking Back

By the end of December 1943, the 10th and last P-47 unit joined 8th Fighter Command. The original six groups had been reinforced in October 1943 by the 356th Fighter Group and December 1943 had seen the first combat operations of the 359th and 358th Fighter Groups. The tenth unit, the 361st Fighter Group took up station in December 1943, but did not begin its combat operations until January 1944.

Meanwhile, the P-51 Mustang had arrived and begun operations from England in December 1943. Its range, speed and manoeuverability brought it immediate success. In the ensuing months the Mustang began to take over the escort duties of the Thunderbolt, but the rugged old P-47 continued to take the fight to the Luftwaffe throughout the great air battles of early 1944 until final air supremacy had been won. Like a good Rugby forward or a blocking back in American football — the Thunderbolt was the aircraft that cleared the path and made so many of the successes of the Mustang possible.

January 1944 saw a change in the escort tactics of 8th Fighter Command. The arrival of the P-51s and availability of long range P-38s made it possible for them to provide penetration support for the bombers to any target in Germany. This left the veteran Thunderbolt groups to be utilised in those areas where interception enroute or on return was most likely. Thunderbolt strength in 8th Fighter Command was at its peak during this period and practically all bomber missions during January were supported by over 500 P-47s. February saw over 600 Thunderbolts take to the skies over England when the first P-47 Groups of the tactical 9th Air Force were assigned to carry out escort missions with the 8th.

Although the veteran 4th Fighter Group had never been happy with the P-47, it continued to fly the aircraft in combat until the end of February 1944. The 4th Group had one of its better days in the Thunderbolt on January 14th, 1944, when it met the Luftwaffe over France. On that day 4th Group aircraft were patrolling the French coast where the bombers were striking the V-1 or 'Buzz-bomb' sites.

The 336th Fighter Squadron was flying a free-lance patrol south of Margny when they sighted the enemy. Captain Don S. Gentile, who was to become one of the top scoring aces of the 8th Air Force, was to demonstrate just what could be performed in the way of manoeuverability in the Thunderbolt at low altitude.

"I saw and reported a gaggle of 15 190s flying East, some 3 000 feet below," Gentile reported. "I took my section down. As we went down the 190s split fan shaped into two groups. I picked two stragglers flying north and attacked at 8 o'clock to the enemy, which were in a fifty degree dive. I closed in to about 300 yards and fired a long burst at the number two 190 and observed strikes around the left side of the cockpit, after which I saw smoke come out. He rolled over at 8 000 feet very slowly and went into a spiral dive vertically. He crashed in open country.

"I slid over immediately back of the number one 190 and closed in to about 250 yards and started firing, closing to about 150 yards. We were in a very shallow dive from 4 000 feet. I observed strikes around the cockpit and engine. As I was trying to follow him down in his slipstream to get another shot, he hit the woods and I pulled out just missing the trees myself.

"Just as I pulled up I was jumped by two 190s and the fun really started. The number one 190 was so close to me that I heard his guns and then he hit me. I broke and the first 190 went over me. I stayed in a port turn because the number two was still coming in, but he was not firing. In the meantime the number one had pulled up sharply to position himself for another attack, but I quickly swung to starboard and fired a short burst at the number two, whom I never saw again. All this action

Poised and ready to go is the green nosed Thunderbolt of Captain Ray S. Wetmore of the 370th Fighter Squadron, 359th Fighter Group. Note the mission symbols forward of the cockpit and the eight crosses outlined below the cockpit.

took place at tree top height. I swung port to get away from number one who was firing, but giving too much deflection as his tracer was going in front of me. I used the last of my ammo on the last burst at the number two 190. I was trying to out-turn him but he stayed inside me. I suddenly flicked and just about wiped' myself out on the trees. Recovering, I reversed my turn to starboard and there he was, still inside me and still shooting like hell.

"I kept on turning and skidding — all I could do. He slid under and overshot, and I reversed again to port. We met head-on and he was still firing. For the next ten minutes we kept reversing turns from head-on attacks, trying to get on each other's tails. The last time he came in he didn't shoot; so he must have been out of ammunition. He then left and I felt like getting out and doing the rumba. All my temperatures were in the red; so I climbed up slowly and came home."

Four other FW 190s were destroyed by members of the 336th Squadron while the pilots of the 334th Squadron engaged another formation of 12 FW 190s and shot four of them from the sky, giving the 4th Group a total of ten FW 190s for the day.

On January 29th, 1944, the Eighth Air Force launched its largest bomber force to date against targets in the Frankfurt area. Very aggressive enemy opposition was encountered and the fighters of the 8th Fighter Command claimed 42 of the enemy destroyed while losing 14 of their own.

Leading a flight of P-47s which were giving cover to the bombers on their way home was another fighter pilot who was destined to become one of the top aces of the 8th Air Force, Captain George E. Preddy, of the 352nd Group.

Preddy stated: "We were flying along at 24 000 feet, with Lt Whisner on my wing, and Lts McKahon, McPherson and Nutter in the second element. Not having seen any enemy aircraft so far on the trip, I kept twisting my head, just to make sure there were none around. Sure enough, ahead of us and below, was a pair of Focke Wulfs, coming in on a box of B-24 Liberators.

"Whisner and I headed for the two bandits, with the other members of the flight covering us. Whisner got his man first, giving him a long burst. His victim caught fire and started to spin. It took a little longer to get the range on my 190. But I finally clipped him in the tail. He started to smoke badly, and I followed him down to 1 500 feet, where I saw him falling through the overcast, out of control.

"Whisner, who had followed me all the way, and I were alone now. We were separated from the rest of our flight, so we started for home. Neither of us had much gas left and we were practically out of ammunition.

"We stayed at about 1 500 feet, flying across Belgium, heading for the Channel and home. When boom! Guns opened all over the ground below us. We were in an industrial area, which was pretty darn well protected by all sizes and shapes of guns. Whisner and I tried some evasive action, but evidently I didn't fly evasively enough. My ship was hit by flak and started smoking badly from the tail. Also, smoke started to fill the cockpit.

"I asked Whisner how he was doing and he said ok. I said, 'Well, I ain't. I'm smoking.' I told him to keep with me, as I didn't think my plane would make it across the Channel. Just before I left the ship I let out with some more 'Maydays'. I then called in and said I was jumping and by this time, with me and Whisner having called in, they were able to get a pretty good fix on me.

"I hit the silk. The chute opened easily and quickly enough, though I don't recall counting to ten before pulling the ripcord, the way it says in the book. The Thunderbolt, by the way, went in about a quarter of a mile from where I landed.

"I hit the water and went six feet under — but I came right up again. I had undone the leg straps of my chute before I landed, so I was able to move around pretty freely, though a gust of wind caught the 'chute when I came to the surface and carried me a little way.

"I inflated my Mae West as I came to the surface and started to inflate my dinghy, which I always wear at the seat of my trousers. I guess I was over anxious, for I tried to do several things at once — and wasn't getting the dinghy inflated. After the proper number of cuss words, I found the right valve, pulled the pin and then pulled another valve, which does the inflating. I guess it took me close to ten minutes to get it blown up, and then it was only inflated about three-quarters of the way. I crawled in, threw out my anchor, and started to bail with the canvas bucket which is part of the dinghy equipment."

Preddy used his signal flares in an attempt to draw the attention of passing aircraft, but whether or not they were seen is not known. Finally, a Thunderbolt from his unit found him and orbited over his dinghy until an RAF air sea rescue Walrus amphibian aircraft came out to pick him up.

Major George E. Preddy scored his first victories flying Thunderbolts, survived a bale-out from one over the English Channel and went on to become a top-scoring P-51 ace.

Upgrading the P-47

Left: 4th Fighter Group P-47 carrying one of the metal 75 gallon drop tanks. This aircraft 'QP-V' belonged to Major Thomas Andrews, CO of the 334th Fighter Squadron.

Below: 'Rozzie Geth II' the personal aircraft of Major Fred Christensen. The P47-25-RE was fitted with the bubble canopy which gave 360° vision to the pilot and was fitted with the Hamilton Standard propeller whose paddle blades greatly increased the rate of climb.

The early matching of the Thunderbolt against the Focke Wulf 190 has already been related. Later models of the P-47 saw many changes which vastly improved the performance of the aircraft. Just how much the Thunderbolt's performance improved will be noted in the following test results:

Relative Data
(1). **Altitudes.** Climb and acceleration tests were performed to 15 000 feet. Other flying characteristics were checked in flights between sea level and 10 000 feet.
(2). **Aircraft employed.** The airplanes used in the tests were a P-47D4 with combat load and an FW 190 with two loaded cannons mounted in the wings and two loaded 30 calibre machine guns, firing through the propeller. The P-47 was equipped with water injection. The FW 190 was in exceptionally good condition for a captured airplane, and developed 42 inches (manifold pressure) on take-off.
(3). **Pilot Personnel.** The pilot of the P-47 had nearly 200 hours in P-40 type airplanes, with seventeen months of combat experience and had flown the test airplane five hours. The pilot of the FW 190 had 300 hours in twin-engine aircraft and 500 hours in single engine airplanes, but had no combat experience. He also had five hours in the test airplane. Thus the pilots were about evenly matched.
(4). **Length of Tests.** Four separate flights of one hour each were conducted. All speeds reported are indicated air speed (IAS).

Recorded Results
(1) **Acceleration**
(a) 210mph to 275mph at 2 000 feet. The FW 190 accelerated faster than the P-47 and gained approximately 200 yards during the acceleration.
(b) 210-275mph at 5 000 feet. Results, same.
(c) 200mph to full power at 5 000 feet. The FW 190 accelerated faster than the P-47 initially and gained about 200 yards, but at a speed of 330mph the P-47 rapidly overtook the FW 190 and gained about 2 000 yards very quickly and was still accelerating. Water injection was used by the P-47.
(d) 220mph to 300mph with full throttle at 15 000 feet. Again the FW 190 initially gained about 200 yards, but the P-47 quickly overtook it. The FW high speed supercharger cut in automatically at this altitude, and this supercharger seemed to cut in at lower altitudes when a speed in excess of 340mph was attained by diving.

(2) **Climb**
(a) 2 000 feet to 7 000 feet, starting at 250mph. Both airplanes were pulled up rapidly to the angle of maximum climb and held until an altitude of 8 500 feet was reached. The FW 190 climbed faster than the P-47 through the first 1 500 feet, but the P-47 quickly overtook it and steadily outclimbed it by 500 feet per minute. The P-47 used water injection and slightly overheated, while the FW 190 did not overheat.
(b) 10 000 feet to 15 000 feet, starting at 250mph. Again the FW 190 initially outclimbed the P-47 through the first 1 000 feet; however the P-47 rapidly overtook and reached 15 000 feet while the FW 190 was at 14 500 feet.

(3) **Diving**
(a) 10 000 feet to 3 000 feet, starting at 250mph diving at angle of 65 degrees with constant throttle setting. The FW 190 pulled away rapidly at the beginning, but the P-47 passed it at 3 000 feet with a much greater speed and had a decidedly better angle of pull-out.

(4) **Turning**
(a) Turning and handling in excess of 250mph. The two airplanes alternately turned on each other's tail, holding in the turns as tightly as possible and alternating the turns first left then right. The P-47 easily out-turned the FW 190 at 10 000 feet and had to throttle back in order to keep from over-running the FW 190. The superiority of the P-47 in turning increased with altitude. The FW 190 was very heavy in fore and aft control, vibrated excessively and tended to black-out the pilot.
(b) Turning and handling below 250mph. Turns were made so rapidly that it was impossible for the airplanes to accelerate. In making the usual rather flat turns in a horizontal plane, the FW 190 was able to hang on its propeller and turn inside the P-47. The FW 190 was also able to accelerate suddenly and change to a more favorable position during the turn. However, it was found that the P-47 could get on the tail of the FW 190 by making a figure eight in a vertical plane. In this manoeuvre, the P-47, which was being pursued by the FW 190 in level flight, attempted to execute a series of climbs, slow turns, and dives which would end up with the positions reversed and the P-47 on the tail of the FW 190. The manoeuvre started with a steep climbing turn to near stalling point, followed by a fall-off and fast dive which ended in a pull-out and fast climbing sweep which again carried

the plane up to the stall and fall-off point. The P-47 built up more speed in the dive than the FW 190 with the result that the Thunderbolt also climbed faster than the FW 190 and also higher. The P-47 pilot merely waited for the FW 190 to reach its stalling point below him and turned very neatly on the tail of the falling away FW 190. With its much greater diving acceleration, the P-47 soon caught the FW 190 in the second dive of his maneuver.

(5) General Flying Characteristics of P-47
(a) The P-47 had good visibility in all directions, and had no bad characteristics in take-offs, landings or in flight.
(b) All controls were good.
(c) The nose was too large to allow good visibility for strafing, but with practice, this airplane might prove successful in ground attack.
(d) The inability of the airplane to pull out of vertical dives made low altitude dive-bombing impracticable.

Conclusions
The P-47 with its tremendous firepower is at least as good as the FW 190 at low altitude. There should be no question about engaging the FW 190 in dog fight at low altitude; but it should be remembered that the FW 190 is a good airplane and has advantages at slow speeds.

Improvements were constantly being made to better the performance of the P-47. Capt Carl M. Bremer, the Assistant A-4 (Supply) of the 66th Fighter Wing listed these developments as follows:
"P-47s originally had the Pratt-Whitney R-2800-21 engines, a 12ft 2in Curtiss Electric 4 standard blade, constant speed propeller and internal fuel supply of 205 gallons in the main fuselage tank and a 100-gallon auxiliary fuselage tank.

"This plane has been constantly modified, improved and changed to meet operational requirements. Some of the major improvements and modifications and the order in which they were applied, are as follows:

"A four point suspension 200-gallon belly tank was the first external fuel tank adopted. It was not very practical because of installation difficulties, and because this tank was normally used on operational missions with only 100 gallons of fuel and was never completely filled. This was followed by the installation of air pressurisation with controlled pressure to the belly tank.

"The installation of a 2-point suspension bomb rack and sway braces were more efficient and permitted the use of a 75-gallon belly tank. Later on came the adoption of British made 100-gallon tanks.

"A big step forward was the replacement by R-2800-63 and R-2800-59 engines incorporating the water injection system and the modification of these airplanes and R-2800-21 engines to use water injection.

"The changeover to 13ft paddle-blade propellers and use of both Curtiss Electric and Hamilton Standard Constant Speed propellers, came next.

"Installation of additional bomb shackles on the wings and necessary plumbing in order to use jettisonable fuel tanks.

"Use of 150-gallon drop tanks on the belly shackles.

"Addition of 'bubble canopy' and an increase in the capacity of the main fuselage tank to hold 270 gallons of fuel."

The speedy, high powered P-47-M-1-RE came to the 56th Group late in the war. The engine, which developed up to 2,800 horse power suffered from teething troubles and the war was nearly over when this was eliminated. This is the personal aircraft of Lt Russ Kyler.

Thunderbolts and Big Week

Right: Fine side view of 'Oily Boid' the mount of Captain Robert Booth of the 369th Fighter Squadron, 359th Fighter Group. Fitting of the 108 gallon drop tank is clearly defined.

Below: Too much braking action on a wet runway could bring about an embarassing situation like this. The drop tank laden Thunderbolt is from the 351st Fighter Squadron, 353rd Fighter Group.

For many months it had been the ambition of the 8th Air Force leaders to launch an all-out attack against the German aircraft industry. With the arrival of the P-51s and the P-38s to give target cover and by using the Thunderbolts carrying 108-gallon drop tanks the time had arrived for the concentrated effort. The only drawback had been weather. When staff meterologists gave the word that the third week in February 1944 would be clear over the Continent, the show was on!

This operation, *Argument* as it was coded or 'Big Week' as it became better known, consisted of five massive strikes against the top priority aircraft manufacturing plants in Central Europe. In some instances these missions were coordinated with strikes made by the 15th Air Force, the strategic air arm based in Italy.

The first of these missions was airborne on February 20th, 1944, when the bombers were primarily dispatched to targets at Leipzig, Tutlow, Halberstadt, Brunswick and Gotha. The escort consisted of 73 P-51s, 94 P-38s and a record 668 P-47s. A number of the P-47s on these missions were from 9th Air Force units.

The heaviest opposition was encountered by the 1st Task Force which attacked targets in the Leipzig area. "A"

A highly respected ace who flew with the 56th Fighter Group was Captain Mike Gladych of the Polish Air Force. Gladych had flown combat in Poland and France before arriving in England. His tenacity in combat was something to behold as he closed in on enemy aircraft to point blank range to assure a kill.

Group of the 56th Fighter Group met the most concentrated opposition of the penetration support when 13 Me 110s were sighted attacking the bombers in the vicinity of Steinhuder Lake. Scoring his 16th and 17th victories that day was Lt Robert S. Johnson, whose life had been saved earlier by the ruggedness of the P-47.

Johnson was with his flight at 14 000 feet when the Me 110s were called in. The Thunderbolts went to the attack immediately. Johnson pulled in line abreast with Captain J. B. Carter and saw a large explosion and sheet of flame envelope the Me 110 that Carter had fired on. Johnson fired on a Me 110 as it began to break to the left. Quickly he fired short bursts into one and then another target before one of the twin-engined fighters pulled directly in front of him. The guns of the P-47 took their toll and the Me 110 blew up.

Another Me 110 was seen several thousand feet below and Johnson went down after it. Fire from 800 yards scored on the cockpit area. As the Thunderbolt closed for the kill the enemy sought refuge in a cloud. Johnson stayed with the craft as it broke out beneath the clouds streaming black smoke. No further fire was necessary for the aircraft went into a slight turn and kept flying on into the ground.

The 352nd Fighter Group took on the enemy fighters during withdrawal support and shot down 12 of them. Major Willie O. Jackson was leading the 486th Fighter Squadron that afternoon and reported, "We were escorting the last few boxes out. Due to bomber boxes being scattered, our cover was thinly spread and broken up into individual flights. Our trip was uneventful until we had set course for home and were crossing diagonally over a box of B-17s at 22 000 feet. I spotted seven or eight Me 109s to my right in close formation slightly below. We immediately wheeled to the right and then bounced them from a wingover to the left. However, the enemy saw us and started a turn to the right. What advantage we had was reduced by someone shouting 'Don't shoot — they are friends.' Determined to identify, I picked out one Me 109 and pulled up behind him and to the outside of his turn. Seeing crosses on his wings, I got back behind him and gave him about a two second burst from 250 to 300 yards, and approximately 30 degrees deflection. I saw some strikes on the canopy and fuselage just aft of the cockpit. Since I was using ammunition load of 3 and 2, I probably got some unobserved strikes. I think that either the pilot or oxygen system was hit. The enemy then flipped over and down trailing smoke. My No 2 saw him spinning into the overcast in flames.

"Seeing another Me 109 off to the left, I did not follow the first one down. The 2nd enemy was in a rather steep turn to the right. By getting lined up on him and pulling my nose thru' to about two rings lead, I managed to give him two short squirts. He went into a very tight spiral to the right with white smoke or spray coming out. We were at 10 000 feet, so I pulled up to 14 000 feet and proceeded home."

The fighter escort claimed a total of 61 enemy aircraft destroyed on the mission with the P-47s claiming 36 of them. Only four fighters, including two Thunderbolts were lost.

An attack on Messerschmitt Me 110 plants at Brunswick, airfield at Achmer and Diephol and others in western Germany, took place on February 21st. Luftwaffe opposition did not come up to the measure of the previous day and that which was encountered did not match the aggressiveness nor skill of the earlier opponents.

Of 500 plus P-47s engaged, only 56th "B" Group met with any degree of opposition and this was on withdrawal support. Most of the fighters destroyed went down in fights over Holland where they were seeking to bring down crippled bombers, Captain Mike Gladych, a Polish pilot flying with the 56th Group, downed one Me 109 over the Zuider Zee and then sighted another as he climbed to rejoin his flight. Gladych pushed his throttle to the firewall and then used his water injection to catch it. The 109 flicked over to the right and made the fatal mistake of attempting to out-dive the P-47. Gladych gave it one burst in the dive and was forced to pull out. The last he saw of the enemy was when the pilot fired his guns for some strange reason — or perhaps a dead finger pressed the firing button. The 109 continued into a light mist over the water at approximately 1 000 feet, still in a vertical dive.

Gladych and the pilots of the 56th accounted for 12 enemy fighters in those scattered combats along the coast as they herded the bombers home to safety.

Thunderbolt pilots accounted for 20 of the 33 enemy aircraft claimed that day while losing only two of their own.

When the bombers went to Aschersleben, Bernburg, Oscherleben and Halberst on the 22nd the Luftwaffe intercepted in force and really made a battle of it. The enemy forced home

aggressive and determined attacks upon the bombers particularly during penetration and in the target area.

Lt Col Francis S. Gabreski was leading the 56th "A" Group at 25 000 feet when a huge explosion was observed in the first box of bombers. The P-47s sped to the scene and found the bombers under heavy fighter attack. As Gabreski took his men to the fray he sighted a formation of about 15 FW 190s forming up after completing a pass. Gabreski picked a target and held his fire until 300 yards. When he hit the gun tit the FW 190 broke up and to the left. The P-47 pilot hung right with him in what became a vertical climb. Suddenly, the enemy seemed to buckle from his fire, fell off and went into a vertical dive. Gabreski continued to pump lead into the fighter until it burst into flames.

The leader of the 56th pulled up and rejoined his formation and escorted the bombers "to the limit of his endurance". Other pilots of the 56th "A" Group accounted for another 11 of the enemy as they broke up his formations inbound to the target area.

Leading the 353rd Fighter Group in withdrawal support was the very colourful Lt Col Glenn E. Duncan. His unit not only turned in a stellar performance of escort but closed the act with an out-

Squadron leader and top-scoring Thunderbolt ace. Lt Col F. S. Gabreski, of the 56th Fighter Group. Twenty-eight Luftwaffe aircraft fell before his guns before he was shot down on a strafing mission in July 1944.

standing strafing attack. Duncan stated, "I was leading the group flying with the 351st Squadron. We were supposed to have been withdrawal support for the 2nd Division but due to the abortion of those bombers because of the weather we were assigned the cover for the 1st Air Division. We managed to slow the group down and wait for the B-17s that were late in coming out and finally rendezvous was made with three groups of them. I talked with the bombers on "C" Channel and they said that everything was all right so I made sweeps around the bombers hoping to pick up any enemy aircraft. As we were coming up on Koln I saw several twin engine airplanes taxiing on an airdrome near Sieburg, Germany, so called that I was going down with my flight. I rolled down to the deck and made a pass across the 'drome from east to west, levelling out at tree top height and indicating about 425mph. I saw several twin engine enemy aircraft parked on the field so I lined up on one and concentrated my bursts on him. I saw many strikes on the ships and pieces flying. I continued firing and picked up a a group of soldiers or crew chiefs on a ramp in front of hangar buildings. Several of them went down while the building received full benefit of all the strikes as it was in a direct line of fire. I pulled up over the building and called for anybody that had followed me down to keep low, that there was plenty of flak down there. You could hear it even above the roar of the airplane. As I was about a mile from the airdrome I saw a freight train and so filled the engine full of .50 caliber. Shortly thereafter another train appeared and strikes were poured into it. This was a small donkey engine but it let off plenty of steam.

"Major Holt, 366th Group, my wingman was in a good position behind me and finished up most all of what I started on the airdrome and the engines.

"As we, Major Holt and I, were on the way out of enemy territory flying zero feet I saw a single-engined aircraft coming across in front of me at about 500 feet and passing from right to left. I let him pass, then fell in behind him and closed up to about 50 to 75 yards. It was a FW 190 and he never knew that I was behind him. My gun sight bulb burned out but I was so close that I just squeezed the trigger without sighting. He lit up slowly and his wheels came down as he slid off on his left wing and crashed near a small town."

Unfortunately, the 353rd lost the top scoring ace of the 8th Air Force that day when Major Walter Beckham was hit by flak while strafing the airfield. Beckham's 18 victories would be surpassed later in the war, but when he became a prisoner he was high scorer in Europe.

The third day of 'Big Week' saw the P-47 pilots down 41 of the total 61 enemy aircraft claimed. Eight Thunderbolts fell that day, five of them flak victims from the 353rd Group.

Bad weather grounded all aircraft on February 23rd, but the 8th Air Force was back at it with a vengeance on the 24th. The bombers were split into three task forces to strike at Gotha, Schweinfurt and at targets north and west of Berlin. The latter force was not escorted.

A change of enemy tactics proved to be very successful due to the early arrival of the bombers on the mission to Gotha. The B-24s of the 2nd Air Division were early and some came under attack before the escort ever arrived. Then there was an unusual amount of confusion at the initial point of the bomb run which caused the bombers to be scattered. The 353rd Group did engage a formation of eight FW 190s in the vicinity of Steinhuder Lake and destroyed five of them. The P-47s managed to destroy seven of the 13

Colonel Glenn Duncan, CO of the 353rd Fighter Group, carrying a load of fragmentation bombs on his personal aircraft. His personal markings of a skeleton riding twin machine guns can be seen on the nose.

enemy aircraft accounted for on the Gotha mission, but the damage had been done. The B-24 had lost 33 aircraft.

The mission to Schweinfurt met most of its opposition on the route in to the target also, but fortunately, the escort was there with them. The 359th Group met the Luftwaffe over the Zuider Zee and downed four of them and then it was the 78th ''B'' Group's turn. They destroyed seven of a mixed force of Me 109s and FW 190s attacking in the vicinity of Dummer Lake.

Major Gerald Johnson was leading ''B'' Squadron of the 56th Group's 63rd Squadron when they, too, sighted the enemy attacking in the Dummer Lake area. Major Johnson went down on three FW 190s and as he did so, one of the enemy fighters turned 180 degrees giving him a perfect dead astern bounce from out of the sun. Johnson opened fire at 300 yards and closed to zero. The burst from his guns lit up the entire cockpit and fuselage of the enemy aircraft. It went down in flames.

Lt Harold Comstock sighted an FW 190 outlined against the snow on the ground. He dived down and straightened out about 1 000 yards behind the enemy. As he closed the aircraft broke upwards and to the right; he had time only for a short burst that scored hits on the tail. All this took place at only 500 feet and the P-47 pilot did not see fit to kill his speed to fight on the deck so far from home. Wisely, he climbed and headed home to fight another day.

There was only limited opposition in the target area, so the P-47s fought the brunt of the battles for the Schweinfurt force, destroying 20 of the 24 German fighters felled. The escort also noted that on these missions that few twin-engined fighters appeared and those that did were escorted by single-engined fighters.

The 8th Air Force wrapped up "Big Week" on February 25th with strikes against the three Messerschmitt aircraft production centers of Regensberg, Augsburg and Furth. The force of 755 heavy bombers were escorted by no less than 139 P-51s, 73 P-38s and a new record of 687 P-47s!

Bombing results that day were very good and but for some of the bomber stream getting off course to the south on the route in, the mission would have been most outstanding. When the 361st Group finally sighted the bombers 15 miles off course they were under heavy fighter attack and some of the lead units had been mauled rather badly. Once the fighters arrived and penetration support picked up there was only limited enemy opposition on to the target. The bombers pretty well had it to themselves in the target area and the only attacks outbound were against straggling multi-engined craft.

One of the units flying penetration support was the 4th Group who were flying one of their final missions in the Thunderbolt. The men of the 4th scored five times that day and Captain Duane W. Beeson illustrated that he really knew how to get the best from his aircraft:

"I saw a lone Fortress which had fallen far out to the right and below his formation and two other fighters were making passes at it, so we opened up and dived toward them. Before we could reach them the Fortress slowly fell off to starboard and began to spiral down while the two fighters circled as though to come in again. When they saw us coming after them, one dived away and the other whipped into a turn, giving about a 60° shot. I fired and missed, then, as we had nearly 500mph indicated, I was able to zoom up above him and come down for another attack.

"This time he dived for the deck, giving me a chance to come in on his tail. He was taking evasive action all the way down which made it hard to get a good shot, then he circled around a small town and levelled out along a small stream, so I opened fire at about 300 yards and closed to 100 yards before breaking away. There were good strikes along his fuselage and his starboard wheel dropped down, then as I overshot him, he dropped off and headed toward the ground. I lost sight of him at this point as we were reforming our section, but Lt Monroe says he saw the FW 190 strike the ground."

The Thunderbolts had destroyed 12 of the 26 victories chalked up on the 8th Air Force scoreboard for the final mission of 'Big Week'. Bombing results had been good, but the German aircraft industry showed an amazing ability to bounce back. The effect of 'Big Week' that was really felt and that was to have a very lasting effect on the Luftwaffe was the loss of many experienced fighter pilots during the five days. Their hand had been forced by the massive attacks and losses were incurred in personnel that were irreplaceable.

The P-47 played a tremendous part in 'Big Week'. The big Thunderbolts did yeoman duty on the penetration and withdrawal support and of the total 218 victories claimed by the fighters of 8th Fighter Command the P-47 pilots accounted for 140 of them while losing only 21 of their own. Truly a magnificent feat.

All the Way to Big `B`

Ever since the arrival of American AAF bomber units in England the commanders had been looking forward to the day when they could strike at the German capital in daylight. Concentrations of Luftwaffe fighters at first made it impossible for the bombers to attempt the trip unescorted but the arrival of the new long-range P-51s and P-38s changed the situation. As usual, however, it was to be the rugged old Thunderbolt that would slug it out on penetration and protect the stragglers on withdrawal.

The first briefing for Berlin came on March 3rd, 1944, but severe weather over the Continent caused the bombers to abort. On March 4th, 502 B-17s were dispatched for Berlin but once more a recall was sounded. However, this time one of the combat wings did not get the message and attacked targets in the Berlin area. The P-47s of the 359th Group met with sharp action in supporting the B-17s on the penetration leg. As the Fortresses

were recalled and turned to head for home a large formation of Me 109s and FW 190s was sighted positioning for an attack on the bombers. Although only three flights of eight Thunderbolts were in the area, they engaged the enemy fighters immediately and in combats that ranged from 32 000 to 10 000 feet, downed three of the enemy and broke up their formation.

March 6th proved to be the day that the 8th Air Force had been waiting for. On that morning 730 heavy bombers escorted by nearly 800 fighters were airborne and en route to attack Berlin. The Luftwaffe, too, came up in the greatest force that it had ever mustered. Not only the day fighters, but all night fighter units were committed to the action. In what may well have been the most fiercely opposed mission and certainly one of the biggest air battles of the war, 82 German fighter planes fell to the guns of the escort. Eighth Fighter Command lost 11 fighters and Eighth Bomber Command

The 352nd Squadron of the 353rd Fighter Group on a practice mission over England. Note the planes are formed into flights of four and elements of two. This 'finger four' formation was used for escort duty throughout the war.

Captain Robert S. Johnson
(Left) congratulates Captain
Walker M. Mahurin (Right) on
another victory while the
latter's crewchief chalks up
another cross on the cockpit.

posted 69 B-17s and B-24s missing at the end of the day. The mere fact that bomber crewmen claimed 93 enemy fighters destroyed emphasises the intensity of the attacks on the bomber formation.

With 108 gallon drop tanks mounted on pylons under each wing, the 56th Fighter Group was able to furnish two formations of group strength for penetration support on the mission. The 56th A Group was to rendezvous with the bombers of 1st Air Division in the vicinity of Lingen, just over the Dutch border, at 1125 hours and escort them to a point between Dummer Lake and Nienberg, south of Bremen. North of Dummer Lake about 100 single-engined enemy aircraft attacked the bomber stream and another ten FW 190s intercepted near Nienberg. The 61st Squadron made initial contact and when the opposition's numbers became too much called for help. The other two Thunderbolt squadrons roared to the attack and in the ensuing fight the men of the 56th downed eight enemy fighters while losing one of their own.

The 56th B Group furnished penetration to the B-24s of the 2nd Air Division on the mission. Major Gerald W. Johnson was leading his charges without event in the vicinity of Bremen when enemy aircraft were sighted. "We could see the rear boxes of Fortresses ahead of us being attacked," stated Johnson, "so we headed in their direction. By the time we reached there the enemy aircraft were dispersed, but I saw an FW 190 at about 12 000 feet and started after him. He saw me coming, however, and kept giving me such a great deflection shot that I was unable to get more than a few hits. After chasing him through the clouds for a while, another P-47 managed to get dead astern and destroy him."

Captain Walker M. Mahurin, leading Red Flight of the 63rd Squadron, stated, "At the time of the attack, we were unaware of the actual presence of the enemy aircraft. We first noticed them when we began to see the flashes of the 20mm shells bursting around the first division of bombers. By the time we got into the combat vicinity the concentrated attack had been dispersed leaving the enemy aircraft flying singly and in twos and threes down on the clouds about 7 000 feet.

"I noticed three of these e/a about 11 o'clock to me down low. After considerable manoeuvring, I was in a position to attack one of these, a single Me 109. As I came down on him, he saw me, and after one turn to the left, he headed down for the clouds. I found myself closing on his tail. I fired several short bursts, none of which hit him. He finally disappeared into the clouds.

"When I pulled up from this attack, I sighted a single FW 190 at about 9 o'clock to my flight, heading down for the deck. This German also saw me. As soon as the element of surprise was gone I knew I would be forced to follow him until he straightened out, before I could make a proper attack. We milled around and around in a turning circle to the left, until suddenly, the 190 straightened out and headed for one of the half-mile diameter clouds which covered the area. As he did so, I closed in behind him and started to fire. By this time we were both in the cloud and it turned out to be considerably thinner than either one of us had anticipated. I could still see the Hun, and when I fired I saw many hits on both of his wings, as well as a few on his fuselage. I was close enough to him so that my hits did not converge to a point. I was then forced to break off the attack as the cloud obscured him. This 190 was probably destroyed for I hit him quite heavily.

"By this time the flight had worked itself down to about 3 000 feet and we were darting in and out of the clouds trying to spot more Germans. They were darting in and out of the clouds trying to evade Thunderbolts.

"As we climbed back towards the bombers, I looked over the side of my ship and spotted a Thunderbolt in a turning circle to the left, with an FW 190 on its tail. I immediately called on the R/T to tell the 47 to break left; however, I later discovered that it was a ship from the 78th Group and on a different frequency to ours. I led the flight in to attack the 190, which was all silver and with a large black "V" painted on its side. He saw us coming, because he broke off his attack and began to turn left to save his own hide. I throttled back and closed in behind him, but held my fire until he, too, would straighten out.

"In the turn itself I was only just able to stay with him. Both of us would stall a bit and then recover. However, when I added water I was able to out-turn him and also able to go around the circle faster than he did. I got within 150 yards of him, and stayed there. After we both had gone around the circle several times, he pulled up into a steep climb. I followed and was able to get in a few shots, as we closed on him in the climb. As he fell off, he rolled over in order to pull the old stand-by of the Luftwaffe — the split S. I followed this also, gaining on him in the dive. When he pulled out of the dive he headed

A formation of the brightly camouflage painted P-47s of the 61st Fighter Squadron. Some are light and dark grey and others seem to be in combinations of dark green and grey.

straight for the clouds in the same manner as the other Jerry pilot had. I was able to pepper him soundly, seeing many hits on both wings and fuselage. The enemy pilot appeared to be having difficulty in flying his ship. He made a 180 degree turn to the left, and as I pulled up I saw his canopy fly off and saw him jump over the side.

"We pulled up from the last engagement and started to climb back out. While doing so, we passed over Wesendorf airdrome where the ground personnel fired intense flak at us. We were able to gain altitude, however, and made an uneventful trip back home."

Following the fierce air battles en route and over the target many of the bombers that had been critically damaged began to attempt to make their way back to England. It was up to the P-47s of the withdrawal forces to get as many of them as possible to their destination.

In position that fateful day to help herd the "Big Friends" home was Captain Walter J. Koraleski, Jr., of the 355th Fighter Group. "After making rendezvous with the bombers we took up a position up-sun and high. Near Dummer Lake, I saw two bombers very low on the clouds with six or eight fighters milling around them," the Thunderbolt pilot reported. "I called the flight and started down from 18 000 feet. I saw two Me 109s attacking one Fort, setting one of its engines on fire. The Me 109s attacked the Fort from about four o'clock to it, passing underneath and pulling up to the right. At about 300 yards or less I fired a burst at great deflection as the 109s pulled up. The 109s passed under me in a steep div-

ing turn and I found out later from my wingman, Lt Fortier, that I had hit the lead 109 all over the canopy and wing roots, and with clouds of smoke pouring from it the Me 109 went into an almost vertical diving turn.

"As we pulled up, my wingman, Lt Fortier, called in two more Me 109s on our left. They were right on the tree tops and we headed for them. My first burst missed the number 2 Me 109 but my second burst of about two seconds at 300 yards distance and a deflection of about ten degrees hit him all over the cockpit, engine and fuselage and along the wing roots on the right side. A burst of flame shot out from the right side of the fuselage and the 109 flipped to the right. As I passed over him he flipped to the left and his wing hit the trees and he cart-wheeled into the ground.

"I then took after the lead 109. At about five or ten degrees astern I hit him many times but couldn't get the sight down enough on him because I would crash into the trees. I pulled up a little and went down on him hitting him several more times. Blue smoke started to pour out of the Me 109. I was about 250 yards from the e/a when I ceased firing and told my wingmen to shoot at it and I pulled up to cover them. F/O Barger went after him first and I saw his bullets hit the e/a causing more blue smoke. Then F/O Barger pulled up, Lt Fortier took over and I also saw him hit the 109 several times. As Lt Fortier pulled up I went after the e/a again with one or two guns still firing. I closed to zero yards, I was so close I thought that my tail hit the 109 as I passed over it but later found out from F/O Barger that the jolt I felt was the Me 109 crashing into the ground directly beneath me."

All told the 355th Group's P-47s downed seven of the enemy while covering the 1st Air Division withdrawal while the Thunderbolts of the 361st Group were credited with five Focke Wulf 190s while driving off the attackers seeking to down the crippled bombers. When the final tallies were in for the day, the P-47s had accounted for 36 enemy fighters.

On March 8th, 411 Flying Fortresses and 209 B-24 Liberators were dispatched to attack the VKF ball-bearing plant at Erkner, on the outskirts of Berlin. The main Luftwaffe attacks were concentrated against the lead combat wing between Nienburg and the target. The 56th 'A' Group was near Dummer Lake when three formations of 20 single-engine fighters were sighted. Between this point and Steinhuder Lake a total of approximately 100 single engine enemy aircraft were engaged by the escort.

Major Gerald W. Johnson of the 63rd Squadron reported, "I then got on the tail of another Me 109 and gave him several bursts from almost dead astern. Large pieces were flying off his aircraft and after the second burst he took no evasive action and was slowly going down. I then pulled up over him very close and saw that most of the canopy was gone — large pieces of the engine cowling and forward fuselage were also gone and the pilot was slumped over against the right side of the cockpit.

"Lt Lovett, my No.4 man, was still with me, so we started back toward the bombers. As we did so, I noticed another formation of enemy fighters coming in from the same direction as the first formation. We could not get to them in time to stop them going through the bombers. The enemy would come through, four to six at a time, from above and in front, diving 5 to 6 000 feet below after going through the bomber formation. As they pulled up they would attack any straggler they may have knocked out of the formation.

"We drove off two attacks by 190s on a straggler, but the deflection shots were so great that I don't think I hit either.

"We then started back toward the bomber formation. I was indicating 450mph to close on a Me109 attacking the rear of the bomber formation. At about 300 yards I opened fire and saw hits on the fuselage and left wing. I soon ran out of ammunition. I didn't think I had got him but since we were only about 6 000 feet and he was still going down I did an orbit and saw him crash into a forest near Celle."

The Thunderbolts of the 56th 'A' Group accounted for 16 German fighters in the heated battles that day.

56th 'B' Group was a part of penetration support to the 2nd Air Task Force. When they got the call from 'A' Group that they were heavily engaged 'B' Group moved up and some of them encountered the enemy, but others like Captain Walker M. Mahurin, had to go hunting to find the Luftwaffe.

"At this time, " Mahirin reported, "we were due for a recall, but were reluctant to start out without firing, especially with all the shooting going on around us. I looked over the side of my ship and saw an airdrome which I think is Wesendorf. I saw one FW 190 circling the field to the left . . . I called the flight and we started to attack . . . the enemy now aware of our presence, passed down the runway from west to east and started straight off at

tree-top height. I dropped down behind him and began to fire. At first, my shooting was rotten and I missed . . . got close enough to him to score a few hits on his fuselage . . . the 190 disappeared into the trees. I pulled up to make another pass at him, but he had crashed."

Mahurin made three more passes on the airfield in which he destroyed another FW 190 and probably destroyed a Junkers Ju 88 that was just taking off. All told, the 'B' Group destroyed 14 enemy aircraft that day.

The Thunderbolts were credited with destroying 42 of the total 79 German fighters destroyed during the day's operations. The effectiveness of the escort is indicated by the fact that bomber losses dropped to 38.

The Thunderbolts had shown that they could still "wield the big stick" when it came to tangling with the Luftwaffe.

Hours of sitting on a hard parachute pack had its effect on pilots. Captain Mike Quirk, 56th Fighter Group ace, had the end result painted on the nose of his Thunderbolt.

A damaged Thunderbolt of the
9th Air Force (Unit unknown)

Thunderbolts could take it

There was probably no fighter aircraft flown in World War II that could take more damage and still come home than the P-47. It flew through bomb blasts, exploding ammunition, train blasts, took direct hits in its fuselage, wings and engine and often absorbed all the fire power that an enemy aircraft could bring to bear. Here is a panorama of 8th and 9th Air Force aircraft that were subjected to all this and even to a mid-air collision and still returned to base. (Left) 367th Fighter Group. (Far centre left) 354th Fighter Group. (Far bottom left) 56th Fighter Group. (Bottom left) 56th Fighter Group. (This page) 56th Fighter Group.

Enter - the 9th

Left: 'Magic Carpet', a P-47D-16-RE, was the personal mount of Colonel Harold N. Holt of the 366th Fighter Group. The 366th mounted the first 9th Air Force dive bomb missions against targets on the Continent.

Below: A 9th Air Force Thunderbolt taxis out for a ground support mission while the bulldozer of the aviation engineers still works on the air strip.

In early 1944 a 'new' 9th Air Force was formed in England. The 9th had originally operated in the Middle East but with the invasion of Europe imminent the 'new' 9th was set up to control the USAAF's tactical air arm in north west Europe. Actually the first combat units of the 9th Air Force had arrived in England in late 1943, but the majority did not arrive until 1944. Included in the later arrivals was the bulk of the P-47s.

The first Thunderbolt group to be assigned to the 9th Air Force was originally a part of the 8th Air Force — the 358th Fighter Group. It had arrived in England in late 1943, but when it was decided that the P-51 Mustang was to be the primary escort fighter, the 358th was transferred from the 8th to the 9th Air Force in exchange for a Mustang unit.

By February 1944 the first P-47 groups of the 9th were assigned to reinforce the 8th Air Force on escort duty. The 358th and 365th Fighter Groups saw their initial action in this capacity and in March 1944, they were joined by the 366th and 368th Groups.

March also saw the Thunderbolts of the 9th begin the type of operations that would become their mainstay throughout the remainder of the war in Europe, the task of knocking out bridges and generally disrupting enemy communications. Eight Thunderbolts got the ball rolling on March 15th when pilots from the 366th Fighter Group attacked the airfield at St. Valery with 250 pound bombs.

There was no existing tactical doctrine on how the type of missions were to be carried out so the pilots wrote their own book. In due course, bombing, strafing and bridge-busting were all jobs at which they became proficient. A few had been in Italy where they had flown some dive bombing and ground support missions, but they were the exceptions to the rule. Mostly they had to learn as they went along.

One of the more impressive missions flown by 9th Air Force P47s took place on May 9th, 1944. Each individual Thunderbolt group was specifically briefed to hit gun emplacements surrounding the German V-1 rocket sites on the French coast. The fighters were to attack simultaneously on a wide front and catch the enemy installations in action as the B-26s and A-20s made their run for home after bombing from medium altitudes.

The Thunderbolts formed up and as they approached the enemy coast they could see anti-aircraft fire begin to

blacken the sky. Each squadron picked out its specific target and dove down on it with 500 pound bombs. Catching the German gun crews unawares, they proceeded to cut a wide swath of destruction with high explosives bombs and blazing machine-guns. A few P-47s were lost but many of the guns that had been taking their toll of medium and light bombers were put out of action for good.

As the time for the invasion of the Continent approached the Thunderbolt pilots had two primary missions. First, to isolate the Normandy area the railroads and bridges leading into it had to be attacked constantly to prevent troops and supplies from entering. Second, to ensure air supremacy over the invasion beaches it was the task of the P-47 to engage and shoot down enemy fighters whenever possible. This often proved to be most difficult as the P-47s were usually attacked from above in the course of their primary ground attack missions.

Bridge after bridge across the Seine river was knocked out. Marshalling yards filled with rolling stock became prime targets for bombing and strafing. Hundreds of rail cuts were made. Locomotive busting became a great sport and the P-47 pilots particularly delighted in fill-ing steam engines full of lead and then watching their boilers explode skywards. Tunnel busting was another new art. The pilots would allow a train to get into a tunnel and then skip bombs into either end, sealing the train inside.

As D-Day in Normandy approached the size of the 9th Air Force continued to grow. By May 1944 a total of 13 P-47 groups were operational with the 9th. This massive force of Thunderbolts was to prove invaluable to the Allied Armies in their offensive role on the Continent.

Finally D-Day came — June 6th, 1944. As thousands of Allied troops went ashore in Normandy the air was filled with planes. Many of the Thunderbolt groups of the 9th flew multiple missions that day and German attempts to reinforce their garrisons on the coast of France were subjected to constant attack.

Continuous patrols were flown over the beachheads. It was during these patrols that the Luftwaffe came out to attempt to catch the Americans unawares. In the course of one patrol mission, Lt George L. Sutcliffe's P-47 flight from the 397th Fighter Squadron of the 368th Fighter Group came under attack.

Sutcliffe was flying as wingman in a flight of four under command of Lt Col

Engine change time for a P-47 of the 362nd Fighter Group. The big Pratt and Whitney R-2800 engine proved itself to be a real workhorse throughout World War II.

John Haesler. The Thunderbolts were just finishing up their patrol and had ventured over the enemy lines to do a bit of strafing when Sutcliffe sighted thirty plus German fighters diving down.

"Break left," Sutcliffe warned and immediately the P-47s broke left and upwards, making for the clouds.

"The left turn brought the enemy fighters in front of me," related Sutcliffe. "I got into position and fired bursts at two, turning with them. Two of the Me 109s broke downward, two pulled upwards, one stuck on Haesler's tail.

"They were getting on my tail, too, but I held to my position and squirted the one ahead of me. He broke left before I had time to give him a good lead. I had to break. Three or four were on my tail getting hits. I pulled left and up.

"That brought me in range of the two that had pulled up from my first bursts, just stooging up to fire on Colonel Haesler. I pulled my nose through, squirted twice and they broke away. The action was so fast I didn't see any strikes. I got hit two or three times by 20 mm shells right then. I saw a couple of holes in my left wing as I pulled away in a tight turn. Haesler must have made the clouds for I couldn't see anything of him.

"I went right around in a 180 degree turn, headed on through the enemy formation, firing short bursts. They broke away in front of me. Their attack split and I got through them. I looked around as I headed for the clouds, trying to locate the other P-47s. I saw No 4, Wingman of our second element. His leader had apparently made the clouds, too. He and the Colonel had paddle props, we wingmen didn't."

Sutcliffe put his Thunderbolt into a climbing spiral in an attempt to reach the clouds. "I couldn't get up there before they swarmed me, like moths around a street light. I had to break. No 4 and I had been fighting them separately for nearly five minutes, neither of us able to reach the clouds, when I saw a parachute from

Below: 'Patty' of the 36th Fighter Group, 22nd Fighter Squadron, sports a two-tone paint job. Upper surfaces are apparently olive drab while the rest of the aircraft, other than an all yellow tail, is natural metal.

Bottom: P-47-D's of the 378th Fighter Squadron, 362nd Fighter Group are airborne. A 500 pound bomb is slung under the belly of each. 9th Air Force ground support missions were often very short. Just 10-15 minutes to the front to drop a bomb on a target and then right back to the steel mat runway to start over again.

No 4's plane. It gave me an awful feeling. I've never felt so much alone."

Sutcliffe kept on doggedly trying to reach the safety of the clouds but each time he got to within two or three hundred feet of safety, the Messerschmitts would be all over him, boxing him in and taking turns shooting at him.

"I remembered that first rule of combat, 'Break into them,' and I broke into them and shot whenever I could. One flew right in front of me. I almost rammed him. I was shooting right into him. The action was fast, I'm not sure that I saw very many strikes."

With full throttle and water injection on constantly, Sutcliffe racked his plane around, skidded, banked from one aileron to the other, dived and swooped at top speed, always with an attacker coming in. "It made me mad that so many would pick on one guy. I started making head on passes. I was really belligerent. They don't like the P-47's nose so they got out of the way. I felt I wasn't going to get out

it, and I was determined I was going to take one of them if I had to ram him."

At one instant when he was going almost straight up, two Me109s got on his tail and fired. They scored cannon strikes that tore holes in his left aileron, cut his elevator trim tab. One 20mm shell exploded against the armour at this back, another tore a gaping hole in the rudder.

"In evading their fire, with my controls shot up, I went into a high speed stall and began to spin down from 2,000 feet under full throttle. I thought of baling out. Too low — no time — ground rushing up. I did the only thing I could — jammed my feet up and pulled with all my might. My plane levelled out right on the deck. I nearly blacked out. Really only greyed out in the pullout, but started back up in a tight right-hand spiral again."

At one time, just as he was about to make the clouds, a German zoomed right in beside him and flew close formation on his right wing.

"He was just staring at me, wondering

No, not an infantryman; this is a fighter-bomber pilot of the 9th Air Force. The pyramid tent in the background served as his home and the bomb crate served as his table.

'Miz Frankie' was the personal mount of Lt R. M. Harding of the 10th F. S., 50th Fighter Group. At the time of the photo the 50th Group had become a part of 1st Tactical Air Force and carried a red cowling and a red stripe on the vertical stabiliser.

This P-47-D 'Ol' Moe' was the personal aircraft of Colonel Dyke Meyer, CO of the 366th Fighter Group. This photo was made at Thruxton, England, while the unit was still carrying the white identity markings before D-Day.

what was keeping me in the air, I guess. I could see his eyes. I stared right back. If I'd had a forty-five I could have shot him. Then he skidded to cut behind me and get on my tail. He'd get me sure if he did that. As he skidded again, I did a hammerhead stall right on top of him. I nearly rammed him. My wing sliced over his cockpit less than ten feet away," Sutcliffe recalled.

By this time some of the enemy fighters had apparently used up their ammunition, for they circled and eight or ten made passes without firing. Sutcliffe saw a Lufbery of 10 to 12 Me 109s off on each side of the mêlée about him, biding their time while the attackers kept him boxed in and took turns shooting at him. "Their planes were above, below, all sides of me all the time. No matter which way I broke, I had someone getting on my tail. Each time I broke I would go into a spin. Some of them would follow me down, but I was going down and back up with full throttle and water injection. The spin was a vicious snap spin, too fast and too violent for them to get in a shot. I would jam my feet up and pull. I thought my back and arms would snap. Then I would grey out in the pull out. Once I was barely above the trees.

"At the speed I was going, I had been pulling streamers on my wing tips all the time. They spread all along the wing in the pull outs. Five times I was thrown into a spin from 2,000 feet. Each time I had the hopeless feeling that I would not be able to pull out."

Eight or ten of the Me 109s were making passes, closing in to knock him down the sixth time he climbed upward. One German was just off his left wing, crowding in, trying to force another break or stall. The dark grey mass of cloud was closer. He was almost there. Out of sheer determination Sutcliffe just kept going.

"I knew it was then or never. I was hanging on my prop, about to stall again as I staggered into the cloud. The Jerry turned his belly toward me less than thirty feet off my wing tip and rolled away. I no more than had time to level out in the darkness and realise that I had at last gained a reprieve in the cloud, when my engine slowed down. I thought I had been hit critically then and would finally have to bale out.

"Watching my instruments I saw that my manifold pressure had dropped back from 60 inches, but she steadied and held at 52 inches of mercury. I'd used all the water, my spurt was gone. It had lasted just long enough."

As he had climbed up the last time, Sutcliffe had heard Colonel Haesler on the radio and had given him his position.

Twenty miles northwest, after breaking out of clouds, Colonel Haesler and the No.3 found him. "I was staggering along, trying to save fuel, practically out of ammunition, when I saw two planes behind and below me. I was still so mad I thought they were Jerries and was set to turn into them head on. Then Haesler identified me and called. Was I glad it was them!"

The aviation engineers wasted no time in getting airfields under construction and even on D-Day an emergency strip was carved out. Within the next week, squadrons were operating from longer strips. By June 19th, a Thunderbolt squadron was based on Normandy.

By the end of June a half dozen or so P-47 units were on the Continent, so when the 362nd Group got ready to move in around the 1st July the men had visions of finding a nice homelike airfield in a rear area. After disembarking the jeeps and trucks of the 362nd started rolling towards the front. After riding for an extended period of time, Colonel Morton Magofin, Group Commander, asked Major Theo H. Davis, riding alongside him, "Are you sure we're going right?"

"Yes, sir," replied Davis. "Here's the field on the map, just where the engineers built it."

They kept riding and the artillery fire became louder. Soon the big guns were

firing behind them and small arms fire could be heard ahead. The colonel checked the map again and went a bit further and found himself looking at a concentration of tanks from the 3rd Armored Division.

A major came running over from one of the tanks and asked: "Are you our reinforcements?"

"Hell, no!" said Davis. "We're an Air Force outfit and we're supposed to move on to an airstrip somewhere around here."

"Oh," said the tank major. "In that case, we'll have to move our tanks. This is your strip. But what the devil is the Air Force doing up here a thousand yards from the front?"

Magoffin gave the order to detruck. As the men were taking off their packs three Me 109s zoomed over from the other side of the lines and strafed the column. Four military policemen directing traffic were killed. Everyone started to dig and they didn't stop digging till nightfall.

The Germans shelled the field when the Thunderbolts were taking off and again when they came back from their missions. More shells came in at chow time and every evening at dusk an Me 109 strafed and bombed. The men simply dug deeper and kept the aircraft flying. The P-47s were on the Continent to stay.

Armourer of the 362nd Fighter Group used a couple of 500 pound bombs as a table to work on a .50 calibre machine gun. These men did a tremendous job of keeping the guns firing, making field modifications plus handling a myriad of other tasks such as loading rockets, bombs, etc.

Achtung Jabos!

Bomb laden aircraft of the 404th Fighter Group taxi out to carry out a dive bombing mission. Crew chiefs lying on the wings served to guide the pilot whose vision was obstructed by the big nose of the Thunderbolt.

The P-47 pilots were largely responsible for blunting the German counteroffensive immediately following the invasion. As with other tactics, they had to develop new methods of knocking out enemy tanks. At first the Germans co-operated. In the weeks just after the invasion many of the German tank crews made the mistake of tying cans of extra fuel on the rear or side of their vehicles. This made them a wonderful target for the machine-guns of strafing Thunderbolts. The Germans soon came to realise however that to tie on extra fuel was to commit suicide and the P-47 pilots were faced with the problem of knocking out tanks like the heavily armoured Panthers and Tigers which were impervious to machine gun fire. The problem was solved in part by some of the pilots of the 368th Group 'Thunderbums'. Captain John W. Baer related: "I was element leader in Captain J. J. McLachlan's flight. We found the armoured column that we were to support, but it was strung out several miles along the road and stopped dead. We established radio contact with the leader and he told us why. Around a bend in the road ahead were a couple of Tigers.

"Those Tigers are the biggest and toughest babies on the road. They're more than sixty tons against forty or so for our Shermans, and their main armament is the famous 88mm gun, which is a murderer.

"So when we missed 'em with our bombs we felt as useful as bees buzzing around a boulder. You see it was a low ceiling and we could only get in a short dive and that wasn't good enough and our near-misses didn't knock them out. They started to shuttle fast, back and forth on the road. We flew around and watched them for a while and then I suggested over the radio that we strafed them. We'll bounce them up in to their bellies."

McLachlan related: "We didn't figure it was much use because Tigers and Panthers are lousy with armor. They've got two inches or more, with double that at weak points. But that was a hard-surfaced road and there didn't seem to be any harm in trying, so I said okay."

"The four of us dived at the lead Tiger," said Baer, "in a line with the road and we walked our bullets along it toward the rear of the tank. That meant thirty-two machine guns hosing .50 caliber bullets at point-blank range. We reckoned the bullets hitting the road might ricochet underneath the tank, and those hitting it direct might penetrate the engine ventilator grill in the back or set fire to those extra gas tins it carries outside. Well, as we pulled up and banked around for a look, we could see that the Tiger was in trouble. Little red puffballs and white tracer streams were pissing out of her on all sides. Meanwhile, the other tank was crabbing desperately away, but we went down and worked her over and then watched her split apart like a package of Chinese firecrackers.

"The boys in our armoured column had climbed topside to watch the battle," McLachlan stated. "We could see them dancing and waving their arms to us, so we wagged our wings at them and I told them over the radio they could go ahead."

When the cloud base permitted, the P-47 pilots knocked out tanks, trucks and bridges in dive-bombing attacks and steadily gained in proficiency. As related by Captain Randall W. Hendricks: "Dive bombing generally took place from 10 000 to 12 000 feet. The pilots became quite expert in placing their projectiles but seemed to favor dropping the 500 and 1 000 pound high explosive types. Pull out was usually accomplished at no lower than 1 000 feet with the 1 000 pounders and 750 feet with the 500 pounders.

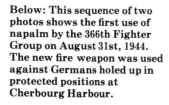

Below: This sequence of two photos shows the first use of napalm by the 366th Fighter Group on August 31st, 1944. The new fire weapon was used against Germans holed up in protected positions at Cherbourg Harbour.

"The primary need for pull out at those altitudes was not only to give the Thunderbolt time to recover, but to avoid being hit by bomb fragments from your own explosives. On one occasion I went after a tank. There was little anti-aircraft fire to oppose me and I held my dive longer than usual. Upon pulling out I felt something hit the aircraft but when none of the engine instruments indicated trouble I didn't think too much about it.

"When I touched down on landing I knew I had a flat tire and finally managed to get things under control and come to a rough stop. After I taxied onto the steel mat hardstand my crew chief told me that it must have been a really 'hot target', for the P-47 had suffered considerable damage. Upon inspection, two very large pieces of the bomb casing were found lodged in the aircraft. One piece of shrapnel had come up through the wheel well and had ripped the tire. A very large piece of shrapnel about four inches wide and over a foot long had lodged in the lower fuselage just aft of the cockpit.

"In dive bombing we tried to initiate our dives so that we were exposed to ground fire for the minimum time. In the course of the dive we would perform either long or short 'S' to come in on the target. This served to throw the ground gunners off the actual dive trajectory.

"Once a P-47 pilot became experienced

Top: Major Robert Coffey taxis out in 'Coffey's Pot', a P-47 of the 388th Fighter Squadron, 365th Fighter Group.

Above: Some missions later 'Coffey's Pot' and its pilot were shot down by German ground fire and this photo was taken by German personnel on the scene.

75

I've been working on the railroad! This was the cry of many of the 9th AF pilots. Here is an example of their work.

he proved that he could do a much better job of knocking out bridges than the medium bombers. The bombers put a walking pattern of bombs across the target and often missed the bridge completely. On studying reconnaissance photos of a bridge we could determine the direction or approach and angle of dive to put the bombs right into the substructure of the bridge to put it out of commission. This we did most effectively."

By mid-July the US First Army had established a line running from St Lô to the west coast of the Cotentin peninsula. On July 25th General Bradley launched Operation Cobra — a powerful armoured offensive concentrated on a 7,000 yard front five miles west of St Lô It was supported by a massive air assault.

Following an attack by over 1 500 heavy bombers on July 24th, the Thunderbolts opened the final act on the 25th with a bombing and strafing attack of the area by eight groups. Another attack from 1 500 heavy bombers of the 8th Air Force followed and then the rest of the 9th Air Force fighter-bombers came in to renew their bombing and strafing. The enemy was then subjected to bombing by medium bombers of the 9th Air Force.

One of the last groups to attack the 7 000 yard long by 250 yard wide strip was the 404th. Captain Duane Int-Hout reported: "There was a pall of smoke over the entire area. It was about eight-tenths smoke up to 2 000 feet, funnelling out toward the north and beyond Carentan, where it stretched eight or ten miles wide, about 12 or 15 miles from the target. The area looked badly chewed up. There was intense light flak in spots, but apparently most of the anti-aircraft had been silenced, used up its ammunition, or burned out its barrels shooting at the heavies."

Tanks, trucks and all sorts of rolling stock were demolished as the Germans tried desperately to flee the area. There were many instances of enemy troops waving white flags of surrender in an attempt to get the P-47s to let up on them. When the day ended Allied tanks roared through the gaps torn in the enemy line by the aerial armada.

And the experience left a more permanent mark on the enemy. "Achtung, Jabos!" became a very common cry of alarm over German field radio sets. ('Jabos' was short for 'Jagdebombers' or fighter-bombers.) The P-47 Thunderbolt had begun to strike terror in the hearts of all enemy troops on the ground regardless of their position or capacity.

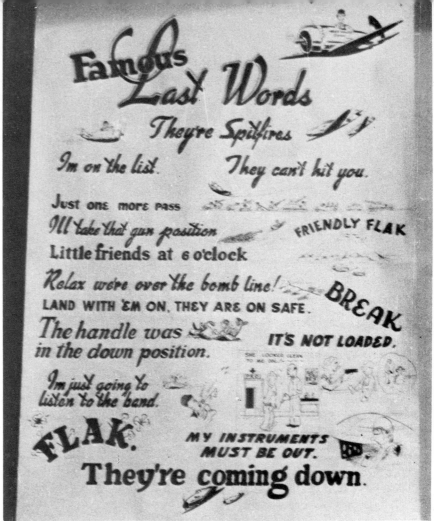

The operation also confirmed that the P47 was the most rugged aircraft that could be imagined. It had brought its pilots back even after it had been written off by the enemy as too damaged to get home. It had flown through debris that would have resulted in the destruction of any other type of aircraft. It even flew into brick walls and let the pilot survive as exemplified by the experience of Lt Robert Goff of the 366th Fighter Group:

"During a dogfight with some Me 109s, my turbo-supercharger ran wild. The manifold pressure shot off the scale, and blew several cylinders. It poured oil all over my windshield, but I could see my wingman only by cracking the canopy slightly.

"He led me back over the lines, but it was obvious I couldn't make the base, so I prepared for a crash landing. But, because I couldn't see ahead, I ran right into the second story of a brick building.

"I was still conscious, and an ambulance driver helped me out of the cockpit — we were in a second floor bedroom — and took me to a field hospital, where I was examined, fed, and sent back to my base."

After the breakout at St Lô, American troops swept out in a great circling move-ment to the east. British and Canadian troops bore down from the coast to form a great pincer entrapping the entire German 7th Army. One escape gap remained — that around Falaise. As the Germans retreated through the gap they were subjected to continuous attacks from swarms of Allied fighter bombers.

Typical of the operations during this period were those of the 404th Fighter Group on the afternoon of August 15th, 1944:

"Colonel Leo C. Moon followed with eight 508th Squadron ships, and after an hour of attacks was being relieved by Major Harold Shook and the 506th when he spotted a highly-profitable target — 20 enemy tanks. He couldn't get the location across to Shook on the radio, so Moon led Pintail Squadron to the target by marking the tanks in a strafing run.

"Shook's bombers claimed destruction of 15 of the tanks.

"By early afternoon the squadrons were beginning their second round of missions for the day— and the 507th finally found the enemy breaking cover and taking to the road north-east of Rennes.

"Captain Tom Weller's second flight got in for a good look at the enemy vehicles— spotted them strung along the

Above left: When the fighter-bomber pilots went down to strafe railroad trains they often had to cope with the flak cars of multi-barrel 20 and 40mm guns. Here is an example of the concrete protected installations.

Above: A 'famous last words' poster that was used by the 404th Fighter Group to keep its pilots on their toes.

road partially concealed by the trees. Weller took some useful steps to stop the flak nuisance at its source on his bombing run. As he told it, 'I saw these tanks and I saw some personnel running about like they were going to man their flak guns. So I said to my wingman, "I'm going down. You stay up here and if they start throwing flak at me, you leap on them with your frags." They must have heard me talking, because I went down and bombed the tanks and they didn't shoot a round at me.'

"Hearing of the concentration, Major Tice quickly rounded up another unscheduled mission and went back later in the afternoon with eight ships, with Weller leading his second element to locate the happy hunting grounds. They found enemy tanks burned out along the road out of Rennes by the previous mission and bombed in an arc from northeast to northwest above the town. They caught five more armoured vehicles, two trucks, a motorcycle carrying five men, and a light flak gun and shot up a scattering of infantry foxholes.

"Major Tice saw a large brownish smoke plume rising from the ground to about 1 000 feet, apparently puffed out through the turret of a tank hit by Captain James A. Mullins. Weller personally accounted for the five men on the motorcycle."

On August 24th, pilots of IX Tactical Air Command caught the Germans trying to escape toward the Seine and knocked

Portable hand-held German 20mm cannon were used to protect many Luftwaffe airfields. These weapons were usually employed in such numbers that one strafing pass had to suffice; the second pass was suicide.

out more than 400 trucks, armoured vehicles and horse-drawn equipment. In the four days from August 24th to 28th, Colonel Gilbert L. Meyer's 368th Group destroyed 426 vehicles and damaged 125. On the 25th, between Soissons and Laon, they knocked out 213.

The big day came on September 3rd, 1944. Roads over the Mons-Cordé canal in southern Belgium were choked with men in field-grey. Trucks, armoured cars, staff cars, wagons and horses were all drawn up, bumper to bumper, nose to tail. Colonel Ray J. Stecker came back from a mission to report hundreds of vehicles stalled in and around Mons. All day long the Thunderbolts and Typhoons swept up and down the choked roads bombing and strafing. By the end of the day at least 1 000 vehicles were burning and mangled along the roads and hedgerows. Strangely, the Luftwaffe put in few appearances while the German troops were being mauled. The Allied fighter-bombers were complete masters of the skies over France.

Left: When the fighter-bombers of the 9th Air Force caught the German 7th Army attempting to escape through Falaise gap they had a field day. This is typical of the destruction that was accomplished.

Below: The Thunderbolts of the 366th Fighter Group caught these armoured vehicles in the Falaise gap and left them all destroyed.

Left: Thunderbolts of the 404th Fighter Group line up for takeoff from one of their steel mat strips. The fighter-bomber units of the 9th AF had to move quite often to keep up with the front lines once the Allied armies broke out from the Normandy bridgehead.

Below left: P-47-D of the 391st Fighter Squadron, 366th Fighter Group gets its guns harmonised. The eight synchronised .50 calibre machine guns of the Thunderbolt were capable of destroying most any German field vehicle except the very heavy tanks and there were ways of getting them with the guns.

Above: A formation of Thunderbolts of the 404th Fighter Group return from a mission. The P-47 closest to the camera is beginning to pitch up into his landing pattern.

Right: The business end of P-47. The gun sight shows up plainly behind the windshield. The windshield of the aircraft was made up of very strong, laminated glass which made it practically bullet proof.

Below: Lt J. H. Wainwright of the 404th Fighter Group was credited with the destruction of six enemy aircraft in one of the most weird combats to ever take place over France. He shot down two of the enemy fighters and another four were destroyed in two mid-air collisions while attacking his P-47.

Lt. J. H. Wainwright

Rolling Thunder

September of 1944 saw the Germans retreating across Belgium in utter confusion. Allied armoured columns were right behind them in hot pursuit. By this time cooperation between ground forces and the fighter-bombers had been worked out to a fine point. American and British fighter-bomber pilots were detached from their units and sent up with the tanks to do the spotting. Their ability to talk 'pilots' language' and direct aircraft right in on the target paid tremendous dividends. At the same time these detached pilots had the satisfaction and exhiliration of actually observing the results of their comrade's work.

An excellent example of this type of cooperation is related by Captain Zell Smith of the 365th Fighter Group: "We were based just outside Paris and our troops were pushing the Germans across northeast Belgium. We would fly up a

The tow tractor or 'cleat track' as it was commonly known, tows a fighter-bomber through the snow during the winter of 1944; one of the worst that Europe ever recorded.

designated highway until we found the air controller whose tank would be displaying orange identification panels.

"On this particular day I had only two of the sixteen aircraft that I was leading bombed up. When we found the head of the tank column on our designated highway I checked in with the controller who told us that they were meeting no opposition but another column some 25 miles to the west was having a lot of trouble. I checked out with our controller and headed west.

"As we approached the area I could see a number of P-47s diving and strafing. As I tuned the controller in on my radio I could hear him calling to the Thunderbolts, 'No, no, that's not it!'

"I called the controller and identified myself and asked him if he needed any help. He informed me that his armoured column was pinned down by two anti-tank guns and that the P-47s that were attempting to help him out weren't doing any good. I told him to tell them to move on out and we would see what we could do.

"These P-47s left the area and the controller called to me, 'Elwood Leader did you see the house they were strafing? It's about a quarter of a mile across the valley and they have an anti-tank gun in the basement.'

"I spotted the house and called to Lt Bob Frye who was flying one of my P-47s that was carrying bombs, 'Do you see the house that has the gun in it?'

" 'No,' he replied, so I told him I would make a strafing run on it to mark it for him. I nosed over in a shallow dive and fired a burst into the house. With this Lt Frye winged over and went into his bomb run. Usually bombs were released at about 1 500 feet but Frye must have stayed in his dive until he was only 700 to 800 feet above the ground. Both bombs arced beautifully through the air and went in right through the roof of the house. When I called the controller I could detect his emotions in his voice. There certainly must have been tears of joy running down his cheeks.

"Three or four of our tanks had already been hit and some were sitting there in the road burning. The hill that they had been climbing was too steep for them to leave the road and go around and they had been trapped like sitting ducks as they attempted to move forward.

"I asked the controller if he had any other problem and he told me that there was another anti-tank gun up ahead. In the meanwhile the infantrymen had begun to move down the road in advance of the armoured column. I orbited the area and looking down at a cross road ahead I spotted a German tank down in a cut across the road intersection. He was camouflaged and had his gun barrel laying right across the road looking down the Americans' throat.

"The controller asked me to call for a bomb strike on it but I told him that the infantrymen were only a hundred yards from the target and I wouldn't let my pilot risk it with them so close. Apparently the controller got in contact with the infantry for they didn't walk back down the road — they ran.

"I then went down on a strafing run to mark the tank. Apparently the tank crew didn't like the sound of my .50 caliber slugs bouncing off their armoured sides for they broke from their location and

Lt V. J. Beaudrault of the 386th Fighter Squadron, 365th Fighter Group shot down the first Messerschmitt Me 262 jet fighter credited to a 9th Air Force fighter unit on 2nd October 1944.

took off across a field. We took turns strafing the tank after my last bomb-laden P-47 missed the moving target. The American column proceeded to advance unopposed."

At this time the first German jets were just beginning to be encountered. The first combat between a Thunderbolt of the 9th Air Force and one of the Messerschmitt Me 262s took place on October 2nd, 1944.

Lt V. J. Beaudrault of the 365th Fighter Group was a flight leader on a reconnaissance mission in the Munster and Dusseldorf areas and was flying at about 9 000 feet to give top cover to other members of his group who were shooting up trains down below.

Suddenly he heard a shout over the radio from his No 3 men, Lt Robert Teeter. "My God," yelled Teeter, "what

was that?" Beaudrault looked around just in time to see a streak flash by his tail and then whip up into cloud.

Beaudrault immediately took his flight up in pursuit. As they headed into the overcast they became separated from the rest of the squadron but they spotted something above the cloud and going into water injection, followed it back down again, losing the other element of the flight on the way. Beaudrault and his wingman, Lt Pete Peters, were left to chase the enemy aircraft alone.

The enemy jet seemed to be playing games with them. Suddenly it sped away from them streaming white smoke from each engine and just as swiftly whipped around and came at Beaudrault with cannons blazing. The Thunderbolt pilot pulled his plane into as tight a turn as possible. The jet went streaking by, travelling

Top: Fast action on the part of the crash crews saved many planes and pilots. This Thunderbolt of the 388th Fighter Squadron, 365th Fighter Group successfully belly landed and has been 'hosed down' by the CO2 foam truck.

Above: Yes, the Thunderbolt did use Malcolm hoods. This P-47-D of the 356th Fighter Squadron, 354th Fighter Group is fitted with one of the English made canopies that were so prized by the Americans until they got bubble canopies.

85

Below: Another example of what .50 calibre slugs can do to a locomotive. The fighter-bomber pilots delighted in catching the locomotives and watching the steam come spouting up out of the punctured boiler.

Bottom: Time was meaningless for the tireless ground crews of the fighter-bombers. Here an armourer loads .50 calibres at sunset on an aircraft of the 410th Fighter Squadron 373rd Fighter Group.

Right: The moment of truth. P-47 of the 23rd Fighter Squadron, 36th Fighter Group takes the arm signal from the officer in the foreground to start his takeoff roll and another mission is begun.

Below right: Thunderbolt of the 373rd Fighter Group is framed by a rack of 500 pound bombs. The pilots seemed to prefer the 500 pound high explosive charges for best results against any number of targets from rolling stock to bridges.

too fast to turn with him. Beaudrault pulled up and waited to see what would happen.

The German came back again and again. Each time the P-47 pilot would wait until the last minute and turn inside him. By this time the fight had worked its way down close to the ground. Suddenly the white puffs ceased to come from the jet's engines — it was out of fuel.

The German pilot went into a steep glide and tried to take evasive action by skidding from side to side. Beaudrault moved in to give him a gun burst. Just as he was about to fire the enemy pilot sideslipped too much and struck the ground. There was a tremendous explosion. The Americans made a pass over the field but there was nothing left but a large fire and shining pieces of metal scattered over a wide area. They headed for home. They had won their first encounter with a Me262.

Although the Thunderbolt pilots were able to gain much satisfaction from their accomplishments in supporting the ground troops, they never forgot that they were all basically fighter pilots. They realised that their job would enable only one or two to tangle with enemy aircraft, much less claim the title of 'ace' by destroying five of them in the air. The P-47 groups of the 9th Air Force usually

flew only one fighter sweep every month or so. These missions presented one of the few opportunities that the pilots had to encounter enemy aircraft and competition to get on the list to fly was very stiff.

This is the description of a fighter sweep as carried out by the pilots of the 365th Fighter Group on October 21st, 1944, as related by Captain Zell Smith:

"Competition to get on the mission was such that as a captain with over 100 combat missions to my credit, the best that I could do was get a slot in the last element of my squadron.

"We took off and formed up in group strength, three 16 ship squadrons. Our mission was to sweep the east side of the Rhine River. The 386th Squadron was flying top cover while the 387th and 388th were down below. I could hear the ground controller begin to call as we crossed the enemy lines. Many bogies were reported at angels 30. A second report told us that the bogies were headed our way. We started to drop tanks and climb to meet them.

"We were still climbing when the controller reported that the bogies should be right ahead of us. I looked up and sighted our top cover squadron just beginning to fly into some cirrus. Just when they appeared to be entering the cloud out poured a host of Focke Wulf 190s almost

An enemy tank destroyed by 9th AF fighter bombers in Holland. Note the classic windmill in the background.

head-on into the top cover. The 190s immediately rolled over on their backs and split essed down on us passing between my squadron and the 387th. As they passed the P-47s of the 387th began to peel off after them. Soon all the 387th was gone and down came another dozen 190s. I rolled over and went down after them.

"I closed on one, got in a few hits and he went through a cloud and I broke off to get back in the fight. My wingman confirmed that the 190 spun on down and crashed.

"As I turned to join the P-47s of the 387th I could see that the squadron was in a terrific dogfight. I looked up and saw another dozen or more Focke Wulfs coming down on the 387th. I was in a position to pull up vertically into them. As I went up I fired my guns and scattered the formation.

"There were FW 190s and P-47s going in every possible direction. It's a wonder that many aircraft were not lost in mid-air collisions in this combat envolving 30-40 aircraft. Many parachutes were floating down through the battle.

"It was most difficult to position oneself to make a kill as you would be jumped as soon as you got into position. I

made two head-on passes that were so close that I could see the white scarfs around the pilots' necks.

"I got a couple of hits but could not press home the attack. I pulled up vertically to get a 190 off the tail of a P-47. I took a 90 degree deflection shot and observed no hits, but the 190 broke into me as I fired at him. As he broke into me he stalled and went into a spin. I did a wingover and watched him spin into the ground.

"I picked up another target and was pressing my attack very close. He went into a vertical turn and I gave him deflection but didn't get hits. I pulled back on the stick to pull the lead up. All of a sudden there was silence in the cockpit. I was pulling so many "g's" my ammunition wasn't feeding. I almost became nauseated at the thought. Here I was in an air battle with the opportunity to down multiple enemy aircraft and my guns were inoperative. I broke off and went out to one side and managed to get one gun firing again.

"I looked around for another 190. Here came five right in front of me. I broke into them and joined the tail end of their formation. As I closed with apprehension, here came a P-47 by with a 190 on his tail. I broke off and scared the Focke Wulf off for him. I joined up with the P-47 pilot, Lt Langley, and went back to the front lines with him. By this time the battle was over. We continued on back to base.''

In the early hours of December 16, 1944, the last great German Counter-attack of the war was launched; the Ardennes offensive. This drive was designed to split the Allied forces and carry the German panzer divisions all the way to Antwerp and Brussels, isolating the northern half of the Allied front. The Germans had counted heavily on the bad weather and fog to cover their movements, but they hadn't counted on the aircraft of the Allied Air Forces — particularly the Thunderbolts.

The Germans moved swiftly and for a time it looked as though their drives would achieve a great degree of success. One of the elite units spearheading the attack 1st SS (Adolf Hitler) Panzer Division. On December 18th two 9th Air Force reconnaissance pilots spotted tanks of this unit speeding towards the village of Stavelot.

The Thunderbolts of the 365th and 368th Fighter Groups took off in four plane flights, each carrying two 500 pound bombs. Twisting through fog to evade the hills which rose to 450 feet, the

first flight located more than 60 tanks and 200 trucks. They dropped their bombs on 30 tanks and shot up 20 trucks before returning to base.

The P-47 groups shuttled four plane flights over the target area until late evening. At the end of the day, the Thunderbolts had destroyed more than 126 armoured vehicles and trucks.

By December 28th the German drive had been stopped. Motor vehicles destroyed by the Thunderbolts were numbered in the thousands, tanks probably in hundreds. Once the fighter-bombers got a break in the weather the enemy was stopped in his tracks.

At this period the 9th Air Force boasted fifteen groups of P-47s. The 367th Fighter Group had given up its P-38s for Thunderbolts and the 354th Fighter Group was flying P-47s in place of Mustangs for a brief period. The sheer weight of numbers of aircraft meant that there was no refuge for the Germans on the ground. Thunderbolts bombed and strafed anything that rolled on the railways and highways. No installations were safe and hundreds of demoralised enemy troops surrendered to the P-47s when they came under attack. The aircraft orbited the prisoners until they could radio ground troops to come up and take them away.

Below: Thunderbolts taxi out over packed snow past a B-17 that has apparently used the 373rd Fighter Group strip for an emergency field. This happened quite often when the 9th got to France and proved to be a most welcome haven for shot-up heavies that couldn't make it back to England.

Bottom: Excellent detail photo of a P-47-D of the 23rd Fighter Squadron, called 'Easy's Angels' for Major 'Easy' Miles, their CO.

Above: Instead of a tower the controller of the 404th Fighter Group uses a make-shift checkered lean-to to direct air traffic at an advanced base in France.

Below: This Thunderbolt of the 365th Fighter Group couldn't make it home to England so it belly landed on the invasion beach in Normandy.

Above right: Religious services were not overlooked even on advanced airfields. Here the chaplain holds church while some of his audience use a Thunderbolt as a pew.

Right: A single P-47 from the 362nd Fighter Group ranges out over England in April of 1944 ready for a combat mission.

Far right: Captain Zell Smith, of the 365th Fighter Group, excelled not only in ground support work, but was very effective in aerial combat with the Luftwaffe.

Thunderbolt Aces

Captain Walker M. 'Bud' Mahurin seemed to have a mania for getting his victories in clusters. When he went down over France and was forced to walk out he had scored three triples and three doubles amongst his 20 Thunderbolt victories.

Above: Colonel Glenn E. Duncan, CO of the 353rd Group, was one of the pioneers of ground attack in the Thunderbolt and once headed a group known as 'Bill's Buzz Boys' who perfected the strafing techniques that were used by 8th Fighter Command. His 19 aerial victories indicate his prowess in that department, too.

Right: First to better the 26 victory WWI record of Captain Eddie Rickenbacker was Major Robert S. Johnson. Originally reprimanded as a loner, he went on to score 28 times while flying Thunderbolts with the 56th Fighter Group.

Below: Major Walter C. Beckham, 'Little Demon' and his faithful ground crew. Beckham rewrote the gunnery manual for 8th Fighter Command and proved his theories in the air by downing 18 enemy aircraft before he fell to ground gunners on 22nd February 1944.

Far right: Major Fred J. Christensen of the 56th Fighter Group was the first pilot in the 8th Air Force to down six enemy aircraft in one day. When he finished up his combat tour he had 21½ German aircraft to his credit.

Below right: Lt Col F. S. Gabreski scored one triple and eight doubles with the 56th Fighter Group and wound up with a total of 28 confirmed aerial victories before he, too, was shot down on a ground strafing mission. Gabreski went on to become an ace once more during the Korean conflict.

Left: A real "dead-eye" shot from the state of Kentucky was Major Gerald W. Johnson. One of the first aces of the 56th Group, Jerry had 17 victories to his credit when he bacame a POW on March 27th, 1944.

Above: Second only to the former CO Colonel Neel Kearby, was Major 'Bill' Dunham of the 5th Air Force's 348th Group. Dunham is credited with a total of 16 Thunderbolt victories.

Below: Captain Joseph Z. Matte was the first Thunderbolt pilot of the 9th Air Force to score four victories in one day — on August 20th, 1944, near Paris.

Right: Lt Quince L. Brown of 76th Fighter Group became the first Thunderbolt strafer on July 30th, 1943. Nearly a year later he would fall to ground fire and be killed by irate German civilians. He was the top scoring ace in his unit with 12.3 victories to his credit.

Final Battles

The Luftwaffe started 1945 off with a bang by launching the bulk of its remaining fighter forces in a surprise attack against Allied airfields in Belgium. The German fighters took off at dawn on New Year's Day and flying down on the deck they headed for their assigned targets. It just happened that as they approached one American base two flights of bomb and rocket laden P-47s of the 366th Fighter Group were just getting airborne.

"We were just taking off for another dive bombing mission," stated Lt. Melvyn Paisley," when one of our pilots saw flak bursts in the vicinity of our base. I was ordered to take over a flight and we

went back. On the way in I jumped an Me 109. Instead of using my guns, I chose to initiate my attack with the rockets I was carrying. I missed him with the first two but got him with my third.

"I shot at one FW 190 at 90 degrees. He rolled over and two bursts sent him to the ground in flames. I then did a half roll and got my second FW 190 with two short bursts.

"An enemy plane then got on the tail of my wingman. I shot at it, noticed several strikes and shook him off. I then pulled an Me 109 off the tail of a P-51 Mustang, knocking him down in one straight pass from above.

"On the edge of our field, I fired several bursts at another FW 190 on my wingman's tail, damaging it. Still another FW 190 came at me head-on and I drove him to the ground in flames."

The Thunderbolts continued to maul the Germans retreating from the Ardennes. Attractive targets were still being offered and there was no pilot more eager to get at them than the commander of the 404th Fighter Group, Colonel Leo Moon. Moon was an eager and efficient commander who believed in getting the utmost from the armament capability of the P-47 with which to destroy the enemy. "I had my guns wired especially so that two on each side could be turned off,' stated Moon. "Many times four guns were enough for some targets. I also carried full ammunition load, which was about 420 rounds per gun. Since I did not believe in returning with unused ammo while there were suitable targets, and I did not think we should be empty either.

This orange-tailed Thunderbolt of the 358th Fighter Group was hit by ground fire and crash landed near Wurzburg, Germany. Note the abundance of American armoured vehicles in the background.

Sometimes there were so many targets that even with the shortest of bursts, the barrels would overheat. Although I had all tracers removed, one could still see the patterns open and become ineffective when the barrels burned out. We then removed the stainless steel barrel jackets from all the guns. Since the four inside guns were most in the airstream and the outside two on each side buried in the wing leading edge, we arranged to turn off the outside ones. Never again did I burn out barrels or run completely out of ammunition.

"We had a bomb at this time which was reputed to be sensitive to almost everything but it was so effective I usually put them on my ship and on others who would voluntarily carry them. This was the larger 260-pound fragmentation bomb and was useful along with the smaller frag clusters to put everyone of the ground 'heads down' when we operated flights in cooperation with tank units against small village resistance points. Sometimes the frags in combination with demolition on the first ship or two opened things up to easy destruction by napalm and even strafing with API ammunition. For example, a 7th Armoured Division commander once told me that our one 4-plane flight burned 90 out of 114 houses/buildings in a village where the tanks were held up by a couple of 8mm guns. After a few minutes work, the 7th walked right in without resistance."

Colonel Moon led a similar mission on January 14th, 1945, accompanied only by his wingman, Major Marshall. "We were pretty anxious to get at the enemy in the Ardennes beyond Houffalize," Moon said, "so I took off with Marshall to see if the weather over the area was clear enough for bombing and strafing. We each carried demolition bombs, a fragmentation bomb and four rockets, just in case.

"Southwest of St. Vith I dropped my wing bombs on two half-tracks, bumper to bumper. I got one direct hit, and one miss off to one side. They were moving real slow on a curve. I came back to make a strafing pass later and they just weren't there anymore. We dropped our belly frags on four or five large trucks on the other side of the same curve, got one direct hit, but they wouldn't burn. I found a staff car, and strafed it. It wouldn't burn. Down the road near a town I found seven trucks and slung two of my rockets into them and they wouldn't burn. Then I tried to fire at a tank with my other two rockets and they wouldn't go, so I strafed it three times.

"I went back to where I'd first bombed, and strafed a third half-track. We strafed the trucks we'd hit with the frag bombs, because they weren't burning. Then I went up and buzzed around a bit, and saw another staff car, painted white, around a bend. I came across it and missed it the first time, so I came back at it from an angle and splattered it. I finally went after a couple of trucks and hit the front one, when my guns quit firing. That's what satisfied me most — to shoot all my ammunition, drop all my bombs, fire all my rockets and destroy the enemy."

By March 1st, 1945, Allied troops were at the Rhine River and on the 6th of the month the Remagen Bridge had been captured. This unexpected capture was exploited immediately and American infantrymen and equipment poured across the river. Not only had a bridgehead been established across the Rhine, but thousands of enemy troops were now trapped on the west side of the river. The fighter-bombers of the 9th Air Force were assigned the task of destroying them.

During the week of March 15th-20th, 1945, the Thunderbolts flew mission after mission to destroy the German Seventh Army. One of the more outstanding records was posted by the 371st Fighter Group. This unit flew 157 missions during the week. They destroyed 1 346 motor vehicles and damaged another 1 154. Their attacks destroyed 180 buildings and factories, demolished 127 railway cars and knocked out 79 tanks plus 26 gun emplacements. Several hundred enemy troops were killed.

Lt Melvyn Paisley of the 366th Fighter Group scored three and possibly four times when the Luftwaffe put on its 'Big Show' on New Year's Day, 1945. One enemy fighter was downed with a rocket.

Although the war in Europe was fast coming to a close the Luftwaffe was still capable of putting in an occasional menacing appearance. One such occasion was April 8th, 1945, whe the 410th Squadron of the 373rd Fighter Group tangled with a bevy of brand new long-nosed Focke Wulf 190-Ds in the vicinity of Hanover. The squadron had just arrived in their target area north-west of Hanover at 11 000 feet when the enemy was sighted. Lt Talmagde L. Ambrose was leading the squadron and vividly recalls that memorable day.

"I heard the call over my radio, 'Gaysong Red Leader there are 20-30 FW 190s at 13 000 feet directly overhead.' I looked up and there were the long nosed FW 190s queuing up to come down on us. I told my squadron to arm their bombs, drop them and to get rid of their belly tanks, too. They were to await my order to break. Red flight would try to cut them in half and Yellow flight was to attack the second half of the German formation. At the time I was quite calm and remember switching on guns and gun sight and checking the yellow pip on the sight and just waiting for them to start their attack.

"They came down on us in waves of four each, line abreast. We continued in our circle and when they were in the right position for attack I pushed my mike button and called, 'Break right'."

We rolled over on our wingtips and climbed up into the middle of the formation. I believe the sudden attack caught them by surprise. They lost their formation and began to break up. I selected an FW off to my left. I started to chase it but he was too fast. I couldn't quite understand it at the time because I had been in combat with short nosed FW's before and never had any trouble closing. He went into a sharp turn to the left and I tried to cut him off but no dice. He kept his distance. I finally had to use emergency power and I started to close on him fast. My wingman was left behind. He didn't know I had switched to emergency power and couldn't understand how I could be flying away from him so fast. With him left behind, an FW got on my tail. I didn't know it at the time but my deputy, Lt D.D.A. Duncan, who was also on emergency power jumped him and shot him down. The German I had selected was a good pilot because it took me five or more minutes before I was able to maneuver into position for a good shot. By this time my wingman had started to use his emergency power and had closed up rather closely, shouting all the time, 'Ambrose, if you don't shoot him down, I will.' I finally was able to cut him off and got in a good two second burst and scored good hits in close on his left wing. He jettisoned his canopy and looked like he was going to bail out, but he didn't. I gave him another burst right behind the cockpit and made up his mind for him. He seemed to have some sort of a seat ejector for he fairly flew out of the plane and as he fell back over my head I could see him trying to open his chute, but it didn't do any good as he flew right into my wingman's wing and his shroud lines were cut through.

"I was now down to about 5 000 feet so I chandelled to the left to gain back the

Colonel Leo Moon's 'I'll Get By'. The CO of the 404th, Moon had his inboard guns rigged so they could be cut off. That way he always had extra ammunition for that juicy target of opportunity sighted on the way home.

altitude that I had lost. I climbed back to around 9 000 feet when two Focke Wulfs pulled right up in front of me. I closed on the nearest one and started firing. The 190 started trailing a thin smoke stream. I scored again and the trail of smoke grew blacker. About this time eight more 190s jumped us and my wingman cried for a 'Break right!', but I didn't hear him at the time. As he broke away he took four of the Germans with him and left me with three.

"I didn't know he was gone until I started to see tracers around my own airplane and felt it shudder as it was being hit. I pulled my plane over on a wingtip leaving the plane I had just crippled. I don't know what happened as I never saw it again. I sucked back on the stick trying to get rid of the three on my tail. I had rolled over and gone into a half split ess as I was too close to the ground to go into a full one but I must not have done a very good job of it for when I pulled out I had four on my tail. I rolled again pulling into a tight circle and saw Duncan coming in on tail-end Charlie who pulled up and away from the fight. This cut the odds down to 3 to 1 which was a little better.

"These guys weren't any too good for in two turns I had pulled up on their tail when I heard someone calling for help. He didn't identify himself and Duncan, who never seemed to get excited at all, called for the pilot to identify himself and give his position. My poor old wingman shouted, 'It's Shackgrove, damn it, I'm on the deck and they're shooting my pants off.'

"I looked down and spotted him with three on his tail. I left the three I was fighting and went down to help him. Duncan got there before me and shot one off his tail. I lined up on the next one and got good strikes on the wings and fuselage. He tried to pull away to the left but my burst hit him full on. I don't believe he knew what hit him for he rolled over and went straight in, blowing up. The last one was shot off his tail by German flak as he flew past a German airfield. They evidently were shooting at the P-47 and didn't give him enough lead.

"Looking around I saw 410 Squadron scattered all over the sky. There were P-47s in one and two fighting in all directions and more black crosses than I cared to see. I climbed back to 10 000 feet and cleared my tail. I spotted four 190s just below me. I rolled over and pulled in back of them and got a good strike on the last one. Just as he burst into flames, I saw something coming towards me from my right.

"I looked up and saw it was a 190 coming straight for me, shooting as he came

Left: Armourers load the guns of the P-47 flown by Lt Talmadge Ambrose of the 410th Fighter Squadron 373rd Fighter Group.

Below: Lt Talmadge Ambrose shows Lt D. D. A. Duncan how he got his four victories in the big dogfight of 8th April 1945.

Above: Remains of a P-47 destroyed by German fighters on the New Year's Day raid of 1945. This Thunderbolt belonged to the 365th Fighter Group which was based at Metz/Frescaty, Belgium at the time.

Above right: Thunderbolts of the 410th Fighter Squadron taxi out for another mission during April 1945. Note that most all P-47s are new bubble canopy "D" models by this time.

Right: Colonel Edwin Chickering, CO of the 367th Fighter Group, out and about in a new P-47-D-30-RA, in the spring of 1945. The 367th was a veteran P-38 unit that converted to P-47s late in the war.

with no deflection whatsoever. I couldn't believe he was going to ram me but he certainly was. I pushed forward on the stick so hard my head banged against the canopy. He just missed me and I could hear his guns firing and the roar of his engine as he passed directly overhead. I was quite shaken up over having someone try to ram me and flew straight and level for just a little too long. I was bounced again by three FW 190s. These fellows were poor pilots at best for in just two turns I closed on their tails and raked the last one from nose to tail. He rolled over into a tight turn and went into a high speed stall and crashed.

"I had built up excess speed in following him down so I climbed up into an Immelman turn to gain back as much altitude as soon as possible but to no avail. As soon as I rolled out I again was bounced by 190s. They were manoeuvring to box me in so I dropped my wing into a tight turn, so tight that I started to grey out. When I could hold it no longer, I slackened up in my turn only to have cannon shells fly past my wing. I barrel rolled but no good. I had lost all but one of the Germans and he was sticking to me like glue. I started to realise that this time I

was fighting a pilot that was far better than I. Everything that I was doing, he was doing better.

"About this time we were all running low on gas. I could hear various members of 410 Squadron saying they were setting course for home. I was alone and knew I had to do something quick. I rolled over on my back regardless of the altitude and started a split ess. I could feel my speed build up at a dizzy rate and when I pulled out I was at tree top level but the German was still there and firing. In final desperation I rolled over on my back, kicked my rudder to slow down and chopped my throttle. He wasn't expecting this for when I rolled back over to level flight there he was flying on my right wing both of us looking eye-to-eye. I noticed by my compass we were heading directly for Berlin wingtip to wingtip.

"I wasn't about to turn around and fly away with that man on my right wing. Evidently during the dogfight I had drifted southwest from where the fight had initially started for I noticed that we were approaching the airfield that we had been fighting around. The German took one last look at me, waggled his wings and pulled away. I don't know if he was short

of fuel or out of ammunitioin or if he was just letting me go. Nevertheless, I hit emergency boost and started to climb out of there. As I was climbing for altitude I noticed nine FW190s in a large circle around me but none of them started to attack.

"As I was flying wingtip to wingtip with the German pilot, who I assume was the group leader, I noticed he had two chevrons on the side of his aircraft. The 190s were all brand new and had dark green tails."

By mid-April 1945 the Ruhr pocket had been all but completely destroyed and the Thunderbolts turned their primary attention to covering the Allied armoured columns that were speeding into Germany from many different directions. Wherever the Germans attempted to draw up a line of resistance they were subjected to attacks from the P-47s. The fighters were now operating without the hindrance of belly tanks, running interference ahead of the racing tank columns, and hitting airfields of the Luftwaffe which was showing signs of an important last-ditch fight.

Many of the surviving German aircraft had concentrated on a airfield at Ibgelstadt south of Munich. One of the P-47 units that hit it was the 358th Fighter Group. They lost one Thunder-bolt to flak but destroyed 21 enemy aircraft and damaged another 18. Lt Scherer, leader of the mission, reported, "The first flight strafed the planes parked on the field and the second flight took the ack-ack, which was throwing a lot of stuff our way. They hit a fuel and ammunition dump, and the explosions raised a curtain of smoke between us and the ack-ack. Then their firing went haywire. When we left on the deck, they were firing flat trajectory at us, and a lot of their shells hit buildings in the nearby town."

Such was the confusion that reigned in Germany at the end of the war. Throughout the month of April the enemy continued to hold out and take unprecedented punishment. The Thunderbolts maintained the offensive right up until the end of the war in Europe on May 8th, 1945. The destruction they had wrought since their arrival in France was inestimable; hundreds of tanks and armoured vehicles, thousands of motor vehicles and railroad cars plus innumerable buildings and installations had felt the fury of their guns and bombs. Nowhere in the course of World War II did fighter aircraft begin to accomplish so much in the way of ground support and destruction of the enemy and his means to make war as did the Thunderbolts of the 9th Air Force.

Below: A captured P-47 found on a German airfield late in the war. There were occasions where American aircraft in enemy markings were encountered, but usually the Germans did their best to steer clear of the Americans.

Right: Beautifully marked P-47-D of the 406th Fighter Group after the war in Europe had ended. Note the vertical fin on this 'D-30-RA' model.

Below right: Close up of a P-47D-30-RA in flight over Germany in late 1945. This aircraft is from the 512th Squadron of the 406th Fighter Group.

Right: The 325th Fighter Group used the Thunderbolt as an escort aircraft in the 15th Air Force for a time. This aircraft of the 318th Fighter Squadron is shown with a 75 gallon drop tank under each wing. The 'Checkertail' was in black and yellow.

Below: 'Sack Time Baby' P-47-D of the 87th Fighter Squadron 'Skeeters'. This unit of the 79th Fighter Group flew extensive ground support for Allied armies moving up the leg of Italy.

Mediterranean Thunderbolts

The first P-47s to arrive in the Mediterranean theatre were assigned to the veteran 325th Fighter Group in October 1943. The 325th had compiled an excellent record in the course of its operations over North Africa, Pantellaria, Sicily and Sardinia during the period March 1943 to September 1943. As the Thunderbolts began to arrive at their base at Mateur, Tunisia, they said goodbye to their P-40s.

In November 1943, the 325th was assigned to the new strategic air force of the Mediterranean, the 15th. In view of the fact that their primary duty would be to escort heavy bombers, a complete change in tactics became necessary in the unit's operations. To enable the group to learn the latest techniques which had been proven with the 8th Air Force a detachment of three veteran Thunderbolt pilots was sent out from England as instructors.

The pilots flew numerous practice missions in the P-47 and then ferried their new aircraft up to Foggia Main airfield in Italy on December 9th. They did not have long to wait to fly their first escort mission. On December 14th, 32 P-47s of the 325th 'Checkertail' Group provided withdrawal support for four groups of B-17s which bombed Kalamaki Airdrome in Greece. There were no encounters with the enemy and all planes returned to base without mishap.

Pilots of the 325th fired their guns in anger for the first time on December 19th. The P-47s had furnished withdrawal support to bombers which had attacked Innsbruck, Germany. Captain Frank J. Collins had become separated from this unit and en route home he spotted the airfield at Ancona. Diving down he made a fast pass during which he shot up a Junkers Ju 52. Major Bill Chick, leader of

the 8th Air Force pilots assigned to the 325th, spotted a 200 foot boat at Rozzeto de Abrizi and proceeded to strafe it, but was lucky to get through the flak they threw up at him.

The first enemy fighter opposition was encountered on December 30th during an escort mission to Verona, Italy. A dozen Me 109s put in an appearance south of Aquila and three of them were destroyed.

Numerous escort mission in January 1944 failed to flush the enemy and it took two fighter sweeps to bring up the opposition. A sweep over the Florence area on January 21st encountered six FW 190s, four of which were destroyed and a sweep over the Rome area on January 22nd met with 15 Me 109s south of the city. In a heated dogfight five of the Me 109s were downed but two P-47s failed to return to base.

Then came the big show on January 30th, 1944. For several weeks the 15th Air Force had noted that the Luftwaffe had been getting its fighters airborne approximately 15 minutes before the bombers reached the target. A plan was devised whereby the P-47s of the 325th Group would precede the heavy bombers attacking the four airfields in the Venezia area of Italy in order to catch the Germans either still on the ground or as they became airborne.

Lt Col Robert Baseler led the group of 60 Thunderbolts out over the Adriatic and they flew at altitudes of 50 feet or less to avoid radar detection. When the group reached the Gulf of Venice they pulled up and headed for the airfield at Villaorba. Upon their arrival they sighted over 60 aircraft scrambling to become airborne. At least 20 Me 109s, a dozen Macchi 202s plus some Focke Wulf 190s and Junkers Ju 88s were on their way up to intercept the bombers. Roaring out to escape the oncoming air raid were Junkers Ju 52s, a Dornier Do 217, a Henschel 126 and a Fieseler Storch.

Major Herschel H. Green reported: "We arrived, as scheduled, fifteen minutes before the bombers were to hit. Shortly after leveling out, I spotted approximately fifteen Ju 52s flying at about 1 000 feet. My section of four fighters swung around to get the sun at our backs and then went into a dive toward the enemy. By the time we reached the level of the Ju 52s, they were strung out in such a manner that each fighter could fire at several aircraft as we passed through their very loose and long formation. I was able to down four on this one pass. When we turned for a second attack, they were all either down or in such close proximity

Below: Major Hugh Dow of the 347th Fighter Squadron, 350th Fighter Group poses in front of his heavily laden Thunderbolt. It carries a 500 and a 250 pound bomb on the shackle, rocket tubes and a belly tank.

Right: P-47 belonging to 1 Grupo de Caca, Brazilian Air Force, is loaded up for a bombing mission. This unit was attached to the 350th Fighter Group of the 12th Air Force.

Gaudily marked Thunderbolt of the 86th Fighter Squadron, 79th Fighter Group. The colourful tail has yellow lightning bolts on a blue background.

to a couple of airfields that ground fire forced us away. Some of them apparently crash-landed off the airfields to keep from being shot down. I don't recall the number shot down by the other three fighters. We never did get back to altitude, for by this time, the remainder of the group was meeting opposition and we were kept busy taking care of the enemy aircraft that hit the deck in attempting to escape. I was able to get a Macchi 202 and a Dornier 217 for a total of six destroyed. My section of four fighters was credited with fifteen airborne kills."

The 'Checkertails' accounted for a total of 13 Me 109s, 11 Ju 52s, six Macchi 202s, two Ju 88s, one FW 190, one Do 217, one Hs 126 and one Fieseler Storch in the combat. Two P-47s failed to return, but the pilot of one was recovered.

The 325th returned to the same area at altitude the next day while escorting the bombers and downed two Me 109s from a flight of four that attempted to attack the bombers. As they headed for home a formation of Italian-built SM 82 tri-motored aircraft were sighted and the P-47s got three of them.

The 325th continued to escort the bombers to targets in Northern Italy, Germany, Austria and the Balkans until late May 1944 flying P-47s. At that time the group was converted on to P-51 Mustangs. The 325th flew 97 missions in P-47s and scored 154 aerial victories for the loss of only 38 of its own.

The first fighter-bomber unit to receive Thunderbolts in the Mediterranean was the 57th Fighter Group of the 12th Air Force. It was soon followed by the 79th Fighter Group. By late March 1944, both groups were fully equipped with P-47s. Both of these units phased out of their P-40s and resumed support of Anzio beachhead and the escort of medium bombers attacking the Cassino area. Two squadrons from the 79th Group encountered the enemy in the air while escorting Mitchell bombers on March 17th, 1944, and downed two out of the intercepting force of ten Me 109s.

Tangling with the Luftwaffe was the exception for the men of the 79th, however. This fighter-bomber unit and the other fighter-bomber groups of the 12th Air Force had little opportunity for such action. Theirs was a war of bombing and strafing the enemy on the ground wherever they could find him. Throughout the spring and summer of 1944 they supported the United States 5th Army in its advance up the leg of Italy.

112

The spring of 1944 saw both the 57th and the 79th Groups operations centre on Operation 'Strangle' whose purpose was to cut lines of transportation, supply and communication north of Rome. The 57th Group was moved to the island of Corsica to position them better for attacks on the railroads, highways and bridges. The P-47 pilots of this unit showed their prowess on one afternoon when they knocked out six bridges.

Both groups went out day after day carrying 1 000 and 500 pound bombs slung under their wings to attack the network of railroads and highways over which the Germans had to transport their men and supplies. Shipping off the Italian west coast and harbour installations as far north as San Stefano were attacked.

In June 1944 the two A-36 groups of the 12th Air Force, the 27th and the 86th, received P-47s. Then in July the 324th Fighter Group swapped its P-40s for Thunderbolts. The tactical striking force of the the 12th Air Force was growing steadily.

During the summer of 1944 there were occasions when the P-47 pilots managed to get away from Italy to do some bombing and shooting. Such was an afternoon in July when the 85th and 87th

Squadrons of the 79th Group went to France to attack an airfield. Upon arrival the 85th made a number of passes while the 87th flew top cover and then the order was reversed. When the P-47s set course for home, over 20 enemy aircraft had been destroyed or damaged.

The men of the 79th had also become quite proficient at dive bombing. On another July afternoon they were called upon to knock out a bridge across the Po River. Two squadrons sent 12 planes each and out of the total of forty-eight 500 pound bombs dropped, nearly 20 were direct hits and 20 plus were very near misses. The bridge, needless to say, was put out of action.

In the middle of August 1944 the Allies launched Operation Anvil the invasion of southern France.

Most of the fighter-bomber units of the 12th Air Force were sent to airfields on Corsica to prepare the way for the land and sea forces involved. The Luftwaffe had few aircraft to commit to the invasion area and the P-47 pilots rapidly depleted the numbers of those few with bombing and strafing attacks on their airfields. In addition attacks on railroads, highways and bridges were once more the order of the day.

When D-Day came on August 15th, the

P-57-D s of the 79th Fighter Group return from a mission over Italy. All aircraft of this unit used an 'X' suffix or prefix along with their individual numerals.

113

Thunderbolts were airborne before dawn as described by Captain Benjamin B. Cassidy, Jr. of the 79th Fighter Group.

"We all had coffee and bread and then went down to the line at 0300 for briefing. I flew the 'lady', Major Lee's element leader. Target was a naval gun position on the invasion coast. We took off at 0450 and it was plenty dark! Major Lee knocked down a string of lights getting off. Beck damn near clobbered the tower, but other than that all got off ok.

"No sooner airborne than we hit a layer of clouds. Almost augured in before we broke through. Radio bleating was a new high! We were supposed to observe radio silence, but no one could locate the right leader in the mêlée that existed. Every group in Corsica had its planes in the air and the darkness didn't help matters. However, we managed to assemble and headed out on course.

"We made landfall around 0600 and the darkness still prevailed. There was an overcast at 4 000 feet, but through the breaks we could see the fireworks on the ground. It was something! All types of flares — tracers skipping all over the ground and sky. Big vessels pounding the coast. We finally spotted our target and made our run. I didn't observe hits, but in view of the fact that we were carrying in-

cendiaries, they lit the place up something beautiful. Just before we talley-hoed, I noticed a small fire on one of our ships out at sea. On the run, I saw a great yellow flash and looking out to sea saw that the ship had blown up. Smoke rose to a good 5 000 feet.

"After the run I noticed two large ships, either battle-wagons or cruisers, firing like mad on the coast. It was a beautiful spectacle to see, but I couldn't help but be sorry for those poor lads down there on those ships. They caught holy hell. By this time, the sky had filled with planes ... every type, including the Navy's Hellcats. We almost mistook a couple for some Focke Wulfs in the haze of early morning. The sky was black with our big brothers. So we returned — no e/a or flak, and the invasion was underway."

As Allied armies moved northwards in France some of the 12th Air Force fighter-bomber groups moved with them, but only one was destined not to return to Italy, the 324th Fighter Group. To replace it the long suffering 350th Fighter Group finally got rid of its antiquated P-39s and received P-47s.

In October 1944, the fighter-bomber groups of the 12th Air Force began to use rockets extensively. These rockets packed the wallop of a shell from a 105mm

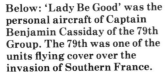

Below: 'Lady Be Good' was the personal aircraft of Captain Benjamin Cassiday of the 79th Group. The 79th was one of the units flying cover over the invasion of Southern France.

Bottom: Red and white candy stripes identified the P-47s of the 86th Fighter Group. This flight is out over the sea, no doubt headed for a target in the north of Italy.

howitzer and were very effective against enemy strongpoints.

In the fall of 1944 the P-47s of the 12th Air Force began flying close ground support missions in cooperation with a ground controller known as 'Rover Joe'. This plan consisted of a controller on the ground, located in an armored car at trouble spots overlooking the front lines. 'Rover Joe' would call the flights of P-47s in and direct them to the ground targets until destruction had been accomplished.

Another innovation coming into use about the same time was a type of homemade napalm. An external fuel tank was carried under each wing filled with gasoline thickened to the consistency of jelly. Two igniters insured the burning of the mixture upon impact with the ground. This weapon, called a fuel tank incendiary bomb, was used extensively against the Germans in their Gothic Line positions.

When Southern France fell it left the Germans with only a few vital routes through which to send supplies and reinforcements into Italy. These primary routes were through the Brenner Pass in the Alps and further to the east the railways from Austria and Yugoslavia. The Thunderbolts went to work on the railroads once more and destroyed locomotives, rolling stock, bridges and made hundreds of rail cuts. During the months of February and March 1945, the Germans made desperate attempts to withdraw troops and equipment from Yugoslavia in order to employ them against the Russian drive through Austria.

Despite bad weather the P-47s flew missions against railroads, rolling stock and motor transport. On March 6th alone, the 79th Fighter Group braved low ceilings and murderous flak to mount continuous attacks on enemy troops and equipment on the move in Yugoslavia. That day they destroyed 28 locomotives, destroyed or damaged 300 railroad cars, 50 motor vehicles, five barges and knocked out two bridges.

By April 1945 Germany was defeated and reeling under Allied blows from all directions, but still refused to surrender. Even the Luftwaffe chose this period to put in some appearances. On April 2nd, 1945, the 347th Fighter Squadron of the 350th Fighter Group, saw aerial action in their Thunderbolts. The unit had been part of the escort for B-25s striking at targets north of the Brenner Pass. Just after the formation crossed the Italian border the controller alerted the P-47s that bogies were on the way and a few

A yellow recognition band outlined in black marked the Thunderbolts of the 57th Fighter Group. This unit became famed with its work with 'Rover Joe' the air controller in the armoured car.

minutes later a flight of 16 Me 109s put in an appearance.

Eight of the Thunderbolts intercepted and did battle with the Germans while the rest went on with the bombers. These eight pilots did a most creditable job in downing six of the enemy fighters. The oddity of the combat presented itself in the form of an enemy "razorback" P-47. Lt Pickerel made an attempt to get the Thunderbolt pilot to identify himself on the radio and when no response was forthcoming he pulled in close and wagged his wings. The P-47 did likewise. However, when Lt Pickerel broke away the unidentified Thunderbolt made a pass at him. Pickerell immediately broke into the craft which split-essed and was lost in the haze.

On a strafing mission against the remnants of the Luftwaffe a Thunderbolt pilot of the 350th Fighter Group won the Congressional Medal of Honor.

Lt Raymond L. Knight volunteered to lead two other P-47s of his unit against the strongly defended enemy airdrome at Ghedi on the morning of April 24th, 1945. The British 8th Army and the American 5th Army had broken out of the Appenines and were in hot pursuit of the Germans who were seeking sanctuary in the Alps. It was imperative that the Allied ground forces should not be impeded by enemy air attack.

When Knight's Thunderbolts arrived over the airfield he left the others aloft and went down to spot the enemy on the ground. Despite very heavy anti-aircraft fire he successfully completed his run. After he pulled back up he radioed the location of the enemy bombers to his fellow pilots and led them on the strafing attack. In the course of the low level mission Knight personally destroyed five of the bombers and his wingmen got two.

On the second mission of the day Lt Knight went back to the area to get the rest of the enemy bombers. This time he asked the rest of his flight to stay at 5 000 feet as flak supressors and then he went in. In ten passes under heavy fire he destroyed fourteen enemy aircraft. During the course of his strafing runs he took an 88mm hit directly in the left wing root.

Although Lt Knight could have stayed in the Po Valley and flown on to British-held Brindisi without climbing he joined his wingman and attempted to make it across the Appenine Mountains to Pisa. The two Thunderbolts climbed to 5 200 feet and started down a 5 000 foot pass. Near the south end of the pass Knight's aircraft encountered violent currents and crashed into the mountains. He was only 25 miles short of base.

The Thunderbolts in the Mediterranean were not lauded by the Press, but the job they did, particularly in support of Allied ground forces, was a brilliant chapter in the Battle of Italy.

Left: Bomb laden P-47s of the 27th Fighter Group cruise above the Appenines Mountains on a mission in support of 5th Army in Italy.

Above left: Major Herschel H. Green applies his 'ace' to his Thunderbolt after the 325th mission to Udine.

Top: Running up and ready to take off from Foggia No.1 are these P-47s with the gaudy black and yellow tails.

Above: 'Little Sir Echo' is loaded down with auxiliary fuel tanks and stands ready to escort the 'Big Friends' of the 15th Air Force to a target in the Balkans, Austria, Germany, Northern Italy or where ever they might chose to go.

Over the Southwest Pacific

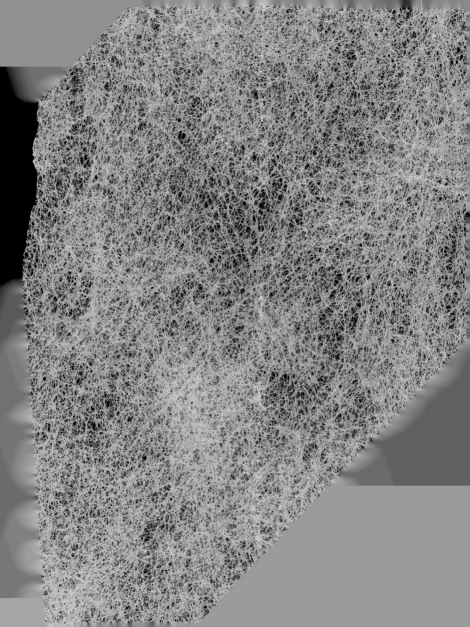

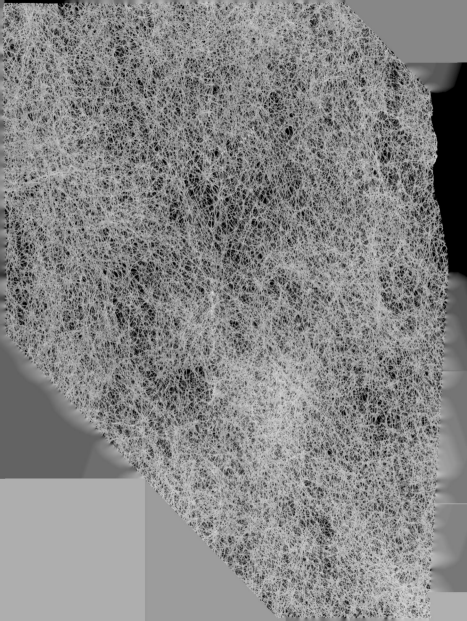

Left: P-47C-5-RE of the 58th Fighter Group in New Guinea. The 58th Group was a real workhorse at bombing, strafing and ground support with the 5th Air Force.

Below: A P-47-D in flight over Australia drops its 75-gallon tank. This aircraft is in new identity markings with its glossy white tail and leading edges on the wings.

The Thunderbolt went to the Pacific theatre of operations out of necessity. With Allied emphasis being put on the war in Europe, the forces in the Pacific were forced to make do with what they had and what little extra they were able to get. Commanders in the Southwest Pacific repeatedly requested new fighter craft to cope with the Japanese, yet few were available. The Curtiss P-40 (Warhawk) and the hopelessly outclassed Bell P-39 (Airacobra) were the mainstays throughout 1942 and into 1943.

The first Thunderbolt unit to be assigned to the Pacific was the 348th Fighter Group under the command of Colonel Neel Kearby. The 348th had originally been destined for Europe but was diverted to the 5th Air Force. The unit arrived in Australia in June 1943 and its aircraft came in by ship in July. As quickly as they could be assembled they were tested and made ready to move up to Port Moresby, New Guinea.

By July 20th all 86 of the 348th's P-47s had arrived in New Guinea having suffered only one minor accident in the 1,200 mile flight from Australia. Immediately the P-47s were initiated with escort missions to Lae and Wewak, fighter sweeps to Wewak and protective cover missions for shipping off New Guinea.

The 340th Fighter Squadron of the 348th Group was the first Thunderbolt unit to engage the enemy in combat — on August 16th, 1943. Sixteen P-47s were escorting transport aircraft to Marilinan when three enemy Zekes were sighted approaching the formation. Major Max R. Wiecks, the squadron commander, turned with one Zeke and fired a steady burst. The enemy aircraft fell away and two other pilots in the formation saw it continue in its dive into the ground.

In practically all of its missions in August, September and October 1943, the 348th Group encountered enemy aircraft. For a unit that was inexperienced, the P-47 pilots chalked up a most impressive total of 51 enemy aircraft destroyed for the loss of only two of their own during the three months.

Highlighting the missions was the achievement of Colonel Kearby over Wewak on October 11th. Colonel Kearby's original plan had been to lead a four plane flight over the airfield and to use the superior diving speed of the Thunderbolts to swoop down on the enemy aircraft taking off or landing.

A flight of over 500 miles each way was involved and the P-47s took off from Port Moresby at 0730 hours, landing at Tsili Tsili for refueling an hour later. In little over half an hour the Thunderbolts were over Boram airstrip at which time they dropped their empty belly tanks. At 1115, still on the way to Wewak, the P-47 pilots sighted a Zeke down below them. They swooped down and Colonel Kearby shot the Japanese fighter out of the sky.

At about the same time Major Raymond K. Gallagher left the formation to pursue another Zeke out over the sea where he destroyed it. The remaining three P-47s climbed to 26 000 feet and levelled off. Soon after an enemy formation of 36 fighters and 12 bombers were sighted approaching from the southeast. The three Thunderbolts went into a steep dive and zeroed in on the trailing flight of four fighters for their first attack. In the ensuing fight Colonel Kearby shot down another Zeke and two Hamp fighters, Captain William D. Dunham, a Tony fighter and Captain John T. Moore another Tony. Then Captain Moore found himself with two Tonys on his tail. Kearby reported what happened next:

"I turned and came in at 400 miles per hour on the tail of the rear Tony opening fire at 1 500 feet. He took no evasive action and burst into flames. I closed for the other Tony which was on Captain Moore's tail but he must have seen me as he turned and dove down in front of me. I opened fire from about 2 000 feet closing in and saw tracers going into him and pieces of his wing and fuselage flying off. I did not see him catch fire nor did I see him crash but Captain Moore saw this Tony burst into flames and crash in the sea."

For his remarkable feat of destroying six enemy fighters in one combat, Colonel Kearby was awarded the Congressional Medal of Honor.

In October 1943, the 36th Fighter Squadron of the 8th Fighter Group traded in its P-39s for P-47s. Although they were only to fly the Thunderbolts for three months, the pilots were most happy to make the change. They had only two opportunities at combat with enemy aircraft during the time they flew the P-47, but they made the most of them.

The first aerial combat came on November 7th, 1943, when four P-47s were on patrol over Nadzab. A dozen enemy bombers escorted by Oscar type fighters were encountered at 18 000 feet. Lt Edward L. Milner latched onto one Oscar and flamed it with a two second burst. Lt Joe L. Clements attacked one of the enemy Sally bombers, closed in to less than 100 yards and downed it with a three second burst. Lt W. K. Giroux attacked two of the bombers after they had com-

pleted their bomb run and scored many hits before leaving them going down in flames. However, Giroux was never credited with these two for he had no witness to see them crash to earth.

Another unit that would fly the Thunderbolt for only a few months was the 9th Fighter Squadron of the 49th Fighter Group. The men of the 9th received the P-47 in December 1943 and made their first interception on the morning of December 10th, 1943. Major Gerald R. Johnson was leading a fight of four up to the American base at Gusap when eight Tony fighters were sighted. Johnson and his flight dived to the attack.

"Our speed was so great in the initial attack," stated Johnson, "that we only broke up their flight. We made repeated attacks, mostly head-on or front quarter. I hit one Tony in the engine and it started burning, the pilot bailed out and an Australian patrol found him. I saw a plane burning on the ground below. This probably was one of the Tony's shot down by Captain Markey".

The downing of three enemy fighters had been witnessed by the men of the 49th Fighter Group on the ground which certainly endeared the "new" Thunderbolts to them. They had another ringside seat on December 12th when nine Helen bombers escorted by fighters made a run on the base at Gusap. Once more the P-47s were waiting for them and two of the bombers and one fighter went down in the vicinity of the base. Another Helen and a Tony fighter went off trailing smoke.

Early in December 1943 the 348th Fighter Group moved up to Finschhafen, New Guinea and from this base it began to fly missions against New Britain. When Allied troops made landings at Cape Gloucester and Arawe, the P-47s of the 348th Group provided top cover.

The Thunderbolts of the 342nd Fighter Squadron turned in a truly outstanding performance over the beachhead at Cape Gloucester. On the afternoon of December 26th, 1943, 19 P-47s were at 12 000 and 18 000 feet when they sighted 15 twin engined Betty bombers and three Tony fighters heading toward Cape Gloucester at 15 000 feet. The 342nd pilots accounted for 14 of the Bettys before they could make their bomb run and just for good measure they downed two of the three escorting fighters. None of the Thunderbolts was lost. Lt Lawrence F. O'Neill had a real field day in downing four of the Bettys himself.

The following day the Japanese tried to get to the ships off Cape Gloucester once more. This time the 340th and 341st Squadrons of the 348th Group were waiting for them. The 340th intercepted a dozen enemy fighters and 10-15 Val dive bombers. Lt Joel F. Pitchford dove on one of the bombers and hit it from the rear at point blank range; it stalled, two men baled out and it went down in flames.

Lt. Myron Hnatio fired on two Vals and saw both of them explode. A Zeke turned into him and Lt Hnatio fired a short burst and the Japanese fighter went down in a tight spiral and crashed.

Major Meade M. Brown dove on a Val which was bombing PT boats and fired at 100 yards. The dive bomber burst into flames. Brown then climbed for altitude and sighted a Zeke below him. A diving pass was made and the fighter exploded.

The P-47s of the 340th Squadron destroyed eight of the enemy dive bombers, seven Zeke fighters and one Tony fighter in the combat. None of the Thunderbolts were lost.

The 341st Squadron mixed it up with a big flight of Japanese fighters the same morning and blasted 13 of them from the skies. The two Thunderbolt squadrons had chalked up 29 enemy aircraft for the day with no losses to themselves.

The 5th Air Force acquired a second P-47 group early in 1944 when the 35th Fighter Group converted its two squadrons of P-39s and one squadron of P38s to the Thunderbolt. Other than a few isolated incidents in March 1944 the men of the 35th would see little air action in their new P-47s until the fall of 1944. Most of their missions consisted of escorting bombers that the Japanese did not intercept, and of ground strafing and dive bombing attacks. In August 1944 the air echelon moved up from Nadzab to Noomfoer Island. From this new base the P-47s of the 35th Group began glide bombing against ground targets on the Vogelkop Peninsular of Netherlands New Guinea in the final phases of the New Guinea campaign.

The third 5th Air Force P-47 group got into action in February 1944. The 58th Group flew mission No 1, an escort of C-47s to Saidor, New Guinea. The Dobodura based Thunderbolts broke in on escort missions covering light bombers up the New Guinea coast, flying patrols up the Markham and Ramu vallies of New Guinea and providing top cover for C-47s and shipping during the invasion of the Admiralties. Additionally, numerous fighter sweeps were flown over the Japanese base at Wewak, but to the chagrin of the P-47 pilots no enemy aircraft rose to meet them.

COLOUR PAGE FOUR
Very colourful 'Snortin Bull, 3rd' of the 404th Fighter Group based at St Trod, Belgium in 1945. / L. Moon

121

The 348th Group had been meeting with more success over Wewak. On March 5th, 1944, Colonel Neel Kearby, who had given up command of the 348th in the autumn of 1943 to take on a command position at 5th Air Force Headquarters, set up a fighter sweep to Wewak. In the late afternoon Kearby took off with Captains William D. Dunham and Samuel V. Blair as wingmen.

Over Dagua strip, in the Wewak area, they sighted three Nell type bombers and came in from astern and sent all the bombers down in flames. The Thunderbolts were then attacked by four Japanese Oscar fighters and Captain Dunham shot down one of these from Colonel Kearby's tail in a head-on pass. He joined Captain Blair but there was no sign of Kearby's aircraft and as they turned for home they saw where a plane had crashed on the opposite end of the strip from where the enemy aircraft had come down. There was little doubt that it was Colonel Kearby's. Dunham's Jap must have got a lethal burst home before joining his ancestors.

Kearby's Nell bomber had been his twenty-second victory.

The men of the 348th Group's 340th Squadron returned to Wewak on the afternoon of March 14th and tore into a formation of Japanese fighters with a fury. The formation of 18 caught approximately 30 enemy fighters of mixed types flying some two thousand feet below them and made the most of their advantage. In the ensuing battle 14 of the enemy were shot down. No American fighters were lost and only three were damaged.

In May 1944 the 348th Group moved up to Wewak and from that airstrip covered the landings and supported ground operations at Biak and Noemfoor. Some enemy opposition was encountered in the Biak area and a few more victories were scored, but generally the summer of 1944 saw little aerial action for the Thunderbolt pilots.

In August and September the 35th, 58th and the 348th Fighter Groups were moved to bases on the island of Noemfoor off the coast of Netherlands New Guinea.

Below: One of Colonel Neel Kearby's 'Firey Gingers'. Kearby was determined that his 348th Thunderbolt group would rank right up at the top and his accomplishment is evident in his 22 aerial victories.

Bottom: Colonel Neel E. Kearby a few days after his illustrious six victories in one combat of October 11th, 1943, with which he won the Congressional Medal of Honor.

From airstrips on this island all three units flew numerous escort missions, fighter sweeps and glide bombing missions against bases on the islands of Ceram, Ambon, Haroekoe and Boeroe to the southwest of Noemfoor; the Moluccas with their main islands of Halmahera and Morotai to the northwest and to the Kai Islands, 350 miles south of Noemfoor.

The 348th Group had not only received new P-47D-23s before its move, but it had been joined by a new squadron, the 460th Fighter Squadron. This assignment made it the only four squadron fighter group in the theatre. The 35th Group, which had also been provided with some new P-47s, had hardly settled at Noemfoor when their ground echelon was loaded aboard ships for the island of Morotai.

In late September and early October 1944 the heavy bombers of the 5th and 13th Air Forces initiated bombing missions against oil targets vital to the enemy in the Balikpapan, Borneo area. Flying without escort the bombers were hard pressed by highly proficient enemy fighter pilots who were based in the area to protect the important oil refineries. In order to provide escort for the bombers some experimentation by 5th Air Force fighter pilots in long range cruise control had to be carried out. By fitting a 310 gallon tank under one wing and a 165 gallon tank under the other, the new Thunderbolts could make the flight from Morotai to Balikpapan a distance of

nearly 1,000 miles and still have enough endurance left to engage enemy fighters.

On October 10th, 1944, pilots of the 40th and 41st Squadrons of the 35th Group took off for Balikpapan. The 16 P-47s skirted round large thunderstorms all the way to the target and when they arrived in the target area they found a heavy cumulus build up to 25 000 feet between Manggar and Balikpapan. the mission report of the 40th Squadron stated: "The planes entered the target area in one 4 plane formation and one 2 plane formation (the 41st Squadron put 10 planes over the target). Planes were sighted taking off from Manggar airfield and the flights united at 20 000 feet waiting for them to gain altitude. Our planes could not go down to the airfield to attack because weather was built up between the target and base. If our aircraft had lost that much altitude they would have to climb over the weather to get home and would not have had enough gas to reach base.

"Captain John R. Young dove from 19 000 to 9 000 feet and pulled up under a formation of five Zekes. He got in a short forty-five degree deflection shot from the rear and the last man in the formation burst into flames. Captain Young pulled up steeply and repeated the pass on the 4th man in the flight. The plane dove down smoking with flames coming from the wing root. A flight of five enemy aircraft tried to cover this plane, but Lt

Capt A. L. Weeks of the 348th Fighter Group in a well-worn Thunderbolt. Weather not only played havoc with the paint jobs on the aircraft, but was much more damaging to intricate electrical and mechanical components.

Above: Rare photo of a P-47-D flown by Lt J. C. Haislip of the 8th Fighter Squadron, 49th Fighter Group. The 8th Squadron was the only unit of the 49th Group to fly Thunderbolts.

Above right: Water, water, everywhere was the accompaniment of fighter pilots in the Southwest Pacific. This aircraft of the 348th Fighter Group is airborne over the seemingly endless vastness of the ocean.

Right: A very distinctive photo of a 5th Air Force Thunderbolt showing the entire leading edge of the wing and the tail in white markings for quick identity.

Strand saw it crash. On Captain Young's second pass, Lt Thomas F. Powell attacked an Oscar in a steep climbing turn to the right. He got an 80° deflection shot from 150 yards. Shots entered the cockpit and engine. The Oscar flipped over and crashed.

"Lt William H. Strand and Lt Hilton S. Kessel made a pass out of the sun, on a flight of four Oscars. Lt Strand shot the No.4 man from dead astern. The engine was hit and the plane rolled over and the pilot baled out. On the second pass, Lt Strand attacked the leader's wingman in a five plane flight of Oscars. The attack was made from dead astern. The plane burst into flames and the pilot baled out. Lt Kessel made an attack on an Oscar during this pass. It was another dead astern attack. Lt Strand saw this plane crash. They climbed into the sun again and united for another pass. A flight of four Oscars was attacked on the third pass. The last three planes split ess or went into a steep climbing turn. Lt Strand jumped the leader before he could take evasive action and made a dead astern attack, firing from 250 to 150 yards. The plane burst into flames, fell approximately 1 500 feet, and then the right wing fell off. Lt Kessel got separated from Lt. Strand on this pass. Approximately five minutes later he called Lt Strand for the position. Lt Strand gave

his position, but he never heard or saw Lt Kessel again. Lt Strand made another pass, but he missed his target on this one. He then had to head for home because of gas shortage."

The pilots of the 40th Squadron accounted for nine enemy fighters altogether while the men of the 41st got three more. Lt Kessel was the only loss.

P-38s accounted for six more enemy fighters and the escort certainly paid dividends for only four B-24s went down that day, three of them to fighters.

On 14th October the P-47s did it again. Fifteen Thunderbolts of the 40th and 41st Squadrons arrived over Balikpapan and encountered large formations of the enemy. This time the men of the 35th Group downed nineteen of the Japanese fighters. The 41st Squadron lost one P-47 to enemy action and one to escorting P-38s. The 40th Squadron had two aircraft crash land on the way home, but both were due to mechanical failure. Only two of the B-24 Liberators were lost on this last big strike at Balikpapan.

Following the invasion of Leyte Island in the Philippines on October 20th, 1944, Thunderbolt pilots anxiously awaited their opportunity to move northwards and take part in the battle. The first P-47 unit sent to Leyte was the 460th Fighter Squadron of the 348th Group. As the bolts flew north enroute to their new base

at Tacloban, Leyte, they escorted B-25s which were out to attack an enemy convoy attempting to reinforce the enemy garrison of the island. Major William D. Dunham, the squadron commander, led his pilots in strafing attacks against the enemy shipping, diverting fire from the B-25s enabling them to attack their targets successfully. Then the P-47s went on to land at Tacloban.

During the month of November 1944, the 460th Fighter Squadron downed ten enemy aircraft, dropped 428 500 pounds of bombs and was reported to have sunk 50 000 tons of enemy shipping. On 24 November Major Dunham led his squadrons against a small enemy convoy, consisting of three enemy transports and an auxiliary gunboat at Port Cataingen, Masbate, and succeeded in sinking all the ships.

In December 1944 the other three squadrons of the 348th moved up to the Philippines. Also moving north was the 58th Fighter Group with its P-47s, but instead of going to Leyte this unit joined a handful of other Allied squadrons on Mindoro. They had hardly arrived when,

on December 26, 1944, a Japanese task force, including a battleship, cruisers and destroyers, was reported heading for the island.

Twenty-eight Thunderbolts of the 58th Group, along with an assortment of P-40s, P-38s and B-25s set out to attack the enemy task force. The planes had no bombs, for their supplies had not arrived, so they had to go down and strafe the ships. The P-47s went out and fired their ammunition, returned to the airstrip between enemy bombing and shelling, rearmed and went back after the task force. They were able to do enough damage to drive off the enemy force. The 58th Group however, lost heavily.

All four squadrons of the 348th Group were operating from the Tacloban area on Leyte during December 1944. The 340th Squadron flew some very effective missions against enemy airfields on Negros Island on the 14th of the month. Captain Meade M. Brown led his squadron on a sweep over Negros and encountered four enemy fighters. Brown downed one of them but, more important, while on the sweep the P-47 pilots spotted ap-

Below: The ground crew of the 5th Air Force worked constantly in primitive field conditions. Here 55 gallon drums are used as maintenance stands in the jungle.

Bottom: Life in the southwest Pacific. Puddles of water from tropical rain in the foreground reflect a typical field maintenance scene for the 348th Fighter Group.

proximately fifty enemy aircraft on the airfield at Silay.

The squadron returned to base for fuel and bombs and was soon airborne again carrying thirty-two 500-pounders. All the bombs were dropped in the general target area and results showed that six twin engined bombers and four single-engined fighters had been destroyed. Three strafing passes took out an additonal five twin-engined bombers and five more fighters. Just for good measure the P-47s also rendered the airstrip unserviceable with four direct bomb hits in the centre of the runway.

All squadrons of the 348th got in on the escort missions to Clark Field on the island of Luzon beginning on December 22nd. The P-47s pilots downed eight intercepting fighters on the first mission and then, on Christmas Eve, really had a field day.

The 348th Group launched full 16 plane formations from all four squadrons for the escort mission to Clark Field. Two P-47s went out ahead to reconnoitre the area with the idea that a pair of fighters would escape notice by the enemy. The strategy proved successful and this flight was able to report that the enemy was patrolling in pairs with single aircraft scattered all over the sky.

The 342nd Fighter Squadron provided close protection for the bombers while the other squadrons split into flights and took on the patrolling Japanese fighters. In the ensuing battle enemy fighters even attempted to bomb the B-24s with phosphorous bombs but to little effect. Thirty-three Japanese fighters fell to the guns of the P-47s that day at a cost of three American fighters. Captain William B. Foulis of the 341st Squadron got three of his squadron's eleven victories to lead the field.

Following the invasion of Luzon and the rapid over-running of the island by American troops in January 1945, aerial opposition all but disappeared from the skies. The P-47s took on the task of supporting the ground troops by bombing, strafing and the use of Napalm. While Thunderbolts had been using some gasoline bombs against enemy troops, Napalm in its latest form proved to be more effective as it caused a flame of longer duration and penetrated more deeply into the dug-outs and caves in which the enemy sought shelter.

By January 1945 all three Thunderbolt groups were based in Luzon. However, in the same month the 348th Fighter Group began its conversion to the P-51 Mustang. In March 1945 the 35th Fighter Group gave up its Thunderbolts. Only the 58th Group continued to fly the P-47 in the clean-up campaign in Luzon. Later it went on to the island of Okinawa but by that time the war in the Pacific was nearly over.

Above left: Lt Hodge of the 348th Fighter Group stands beside his aircraft which is fitted with a large field manufactured drop tank. It may have been crude, but it was serviceable.

Top: When the pilots of the 5th Air Force reached the Philippines there was more time for fancy paint jobs and such as is illustrated by this colourful Thunderbolt belonging to 348th Group ace, Captain Marvin Grant.

Above: 'Razorback Jug' being ferried to a 5th Air Force fighter unit makes an island stop. It is carrying the large 165 gallon tanks essential for long hops.

On to Japan

The first P-47 unit of the US 7th Air Force got into the combat theatre on June 22nd, 1944 when the 318th Fighter Group took off from the carrier *Natoma Bay* and landed on the island of Saipan. Although there was no aerial opposition to cope with the 318th had their hands full. The island was still not secure and a number of times Japanese troops managed to infiltrate the American lines and destroy a few P-47s during the night. Life became quite hectic and the enemy saw to it that few nights were peaceful.

The Thunderbolts did yeoman duty in supporting the US Marines on the island. At times they strafed so close to the front-line troops that they showered them with spent brass cases from their machine guns. These operations also developed the tactics for the efficient use of Napalm.

The P-47s would come in at altitudes ranging from 25-50 feet and drop the Napalm tanks. If they failed to explode they would be ignited by machine gun fire from the next plane.

The 318th Group stayed on in Saipan after the island was conquered and flew missions against other islands in the Marianas chain. These included one of the most extraordinary missions of the Pacific war — on October 21st, 1944. The pilots had been experimenting with long range cruise control in the hope that they could give the B-24s a hand on their missions from Saipan to Iwo Jima, a distance of 1 500 miles.

Twenty P-47s were loaded with belly and wing tanks and took off to escort the B-24s. On the earlier missions enemy fighters had followed the bombers out as far as the Minami Islands. It was at this point that the P-47s were to pick up the Liberators and bring them home. They made the rendezvous, but the enemy fighters didn't come out with the bombers. Only one lonely, twin-engined Nick fighter showed up and it was shot down by Captain Charles W. Tenant. The Thunderbolts were airborne for 6 hours and 38 minutes, a record at that time.

The quest for a long-range fighter had brought about a new and more improved P-47, the 'N' model. The long-range feature was provided by four interconnected fuel cells which were housed near the wing roots which provided capacity for an additional 200 gallons of gasoline. This combined with auxiliary tanks could keep the Thunderbolt airborne for as long as 10 hours.

The P-47-N was also fitted with the R-2800-57 Double Wasp engine which was also used in the P-47-M which saw service in Europe late in the war. Along with an improved engine the 'N' also featured an automatic engine control which would

Thunderbolt of the 318th Fighter Group is airborne from the deck of the USS *Manila Bay*. These P-47s were transported from Hawaii to Saipan where they flew combat mission during the conquest of the Marianas Islands.

Lt Bob Forrest of the 463rd Fighter Squadron, 507th Fighter Group winds up for take off on Ie Shima. The big tank under the wing is filled with napalm to be dropped on targets in Japan.

maintain power settings and an autopilot system to relieve the pilot on long missions.

The pilots of the 318th Group were the first to pick up the new aircraft in Hawaii. Using B-25s as navigation aircraft they ferried their new Thunderbolts back via Johnston Island, to Majuro, to Eniwetok and on to Saipan, a distance of 4 132 miles. Not a single P-47 was lost.

Ironically, the move from Saipan in their new aircraft took them to the new conquered island of Ie Shima just off the coast of Okinawa only 325 miles from Japan.

On May 25th 1945, Lts Richard H. Anderson and Donald E. Kennedy were flying two of the new P-47-Ns over Southern Amami O Shima, a Japanese base between Okinawa and Kyushu, when they saw 30 planes bearing down upon them. At first they took them to be Marine Corps Corsairs and it was not until the formation had passed that they realised that the planes were Japanese Zeros.

Anderson immediately salvoed the bomb that he had been carrying and climbed up to the rear of the Japanese formation. He was still slightly below when the last Zeke in the formation winged over and came down to meet him. Both pilots held their courses, blazing away at each other until at the last second, the Zeke pulled up over Anderson with his engine and fuselage swathed in flames.

By this time Kennedy, too, had downed a Zeke and they rejoined and closed on two more Zekes trailing the Japanese formation. Anderson sent the one on the right flaming into the water. He then closed on the leader, at which Kennedy had been firing, and put the finishing touches to him. Almost simultaneously Kennedy sent another Zeke flaming and arcing into the sea.

Reforming once more, the two Americans eased in on more of the Zekes. Anderson fired and one of the Japanese fighters dropped his nose and fell straight into the water. Kennedy opened up and matched Anderson's feat. Anderson now closed in fast on another and sent it flaming and cart-wheeling into the sea. In only four minutes Anderson had downed five enemy aircraft and Kennedy three.

The 318th was in action all over the Okinawa area that day breaking up Japanese Kamikaze attacks on American shipping in the harbor. The men of the 318th downed thirty-four enemy aircraft in only four hours.

On May 28th, Captain John E. Vogt led a four plane flight over Kanoya at 16 000 feet. As he looked down on the airfields and potential targets below he sighted 28 Zekes coming in from the northwest. The P-47s dropped their tanks and roared up to meet the enemy.

When the fight was over Captain John Vogt had downed five of the enemy while his wingman, Lt LaRochelle, accounted for one more.

In June 1945 the P-47s of the 318th were joined in combat by a second Thunderbolt unit, the 413th Fighter Group. Another P-47 group flying the P-47-N, the 507th, joined them on Ie Shima in July 1945.

However, it was the 318th Group that kept encountering the enemy and adding to its score. On June 6th, Captain Judge E. Wolfe became the first AAF pilot in the Pacific to pick off a Japanese fighter with a rocket.

Wolfe was leading a patrol flight over Kyushu when he spotted seven Zekes heading toward him with a 4 000 foot altitude advantage. Wolfe was carrying two rockets under his wing and was reluctant to salvo them, so he lined up on one of the Zekes and let them go. The Zeke disintegrated.

The primary hazard to the pilots of the P-47-Ns was not the enemy but the combination of the terrain features of Ie Shima and the heavy loads their aircraft carried. The extent of this latter hazard is related by W. Preston Germain who was one of the pilots of the 318th Group at that time:

"Ie Shima was a difficult island to fly from because the runway had a hump in the centre and went down hill towards both ends — north and south — and at either end had a very definite cliff. When we took off on long-range missions carrying two 500 pound bombs and rockets plus the enormous quantity of fuel the P47-N carried, it was a question whether or not we could get off the runway. The pilots we lost were those who failed to get airborne even after jettisoning their rockets and bombs two-thirds of the way down the runway.

"We later solved this problem by stationing a flying officer half way down with a portable radio set so that he could tell pilots who weren't going to make it to jettison their rockets, bombs or napalm tanks at an earlier point. Even then many of them would barely wobble into the air at 108mph sometimes dropping out of sight momentarily as they came off the end of the runway and went over the cliff."

Most of the battles against enemy fighters were over by late June 1945 and the Thunderbolt pilots had to satisfy themselves by hitting ground targets on the Japanese home islands. During this

period they covered a segment with a radius of 750 miles and an arc of almost 2 000 miles extending from Osaka and Nagoya on the island of Honshu in the northeast to Keijo, Korea on the northwest, and westwards to Shanghai on the Chinese mainland.

On August 13th, 1945, the 507th Fighter Group made a 1 800 miles round trip northwest to Keijo, Korea on a fighter sweep which lasted eight hours. During the course of the mission they destroyed 18 enemy aircraft and lost only one Thunderbolt and that to anti-aircraft fire. Lt Oscar F. Perdomo, who had set a nine hour mission record on July 5th, set another for his unit when he downed four Oscars and a Willow trainer to become an ace in a day.

The last Thunderbolt victory in the Pacific was scored on August 14th, 1945, on a fighter sweep of the Osaka-Nagoya area by the 318th Fighter Group. Approximately 10 miles east of Osaka a Frank fighter was spotted at 12 o'clock going away. Captain Currey closed on the enemy, opening fire from 1 000 feet and closing to 400 feet. Tracers were observed pouring into the Frank's fuselage, tail section and cockpit. The enemy fighter whipped off to the right, trailing smoke. Both Captain Currey and his wingman saw the pilot bale out.

Top: A flight of P-47-Ns from the 463rd Fighter Squadron, 507th Fighter Group as photographed from a B-24. The aircraft are not heavily laden, so undoubtedly they are not outward bound on a combat mission. The P-47-N was designed to do long-range escort in the Pacific but took part in very few bomber escort mission late in the war.

Above: An unusual shot of a brand-new P-47-N going away. Note the antennas on the rear. The single is the radio antenna. The dual is for the IFF (Identification, Friend or Foe) set.

Top left: Beautiful side view of Lt Dusty Schlueter's P-47-N showing the markings of the 28th Fighter Squadron, 413th Fighter Group. Heart on the tail was the marking of the 28th Squadron.

Centre left: Sitting on alert awaiting an order to taxi and takeoff are P-47-Ns of the 28th Fighter Squadron, 413th Fighter Group.

Below: P-47-N taken from overhead by a photographer in the belly of a B-24. This excellent photo shows the markings on the wings and tail of the aircraft and also produces the topside view of the 'N' is great detail.

Right: There's nothing like the frame of a dame seems to be the theme of this photo of a P-47-N of the 333rd Fighter Squadron, 318th Fighter Group on Ie Shima.

Below right: Head-on view of another P-47-N, this particular aircraft from the 333rd Fighter Squadron. The broad black and yellow stripes on the tail were squadron markings.

With the Royal Air Force in Burma

By the summer of 1944 the Japanese offensive out of Burma with Delhi as its objective had been stopped. The British 14th Army's counter-offensive had begun before the monsoon broke and the enemy was in retreat. When the rains came the British took advantage of the situation to reinforce and resupply their forces.

The Royal Air Force, too, made ready for the coming offensive. The weary Hawker Hurricanes and in some cases, Bristol Blenheims, were replaced with P-47D-21s or Thunderbolt Is as they were known in the Royal Air Force. The first squadron to obtain the new craft and take them into combat was No 146 Squadron. Shortly thereafter another eight squadrons were withdrawn from the front to Yelahanka, near Bangalore, where they received Thunderbolts before returning to 221 Group in Assam and 224 Group in Bengal.

Before the end of 1944, nine RAF squadrons were flying Thunderbolts with a few of them receiving Thunderbolt IIs which had the 'bubble canopy' giving the pilot unexcelled 360° vision. By the end of the war Thunderbolts equipped some 15 Royal Air Force squadrons in Southeast Asia.

One of the fighter pilots who took the Thunderbolt I into combat in September 1944 with No 146 Squadron was a young Canadian, Pilot Officer A. L. Coombs who relates his initial doubts and later experiences with the Thunderbolt.

"We had our misgivings when we were told that the Thunderbolt would be our replacement aircraft as we all wanted Spitfires.

"We lost about eight pilots converting on to the type as we had no idea how fast it could dive. An American pilot put us at ease by looping off the deck , and then we put it to work.

"We experimented with long range tanks as well as 500 pound bombs. In fact we used it for low level strafing more than its original intent as a fighter. It was the most stable platform we had ever used, especially in a dive from 23 000 feet.

"We had little contact with enemy aircraft, but at first we were escorted by RAF Mosquitos which at the time were rated as the world's fastest fighters. However, when they escorted us, they had trouble keeping up.

"I think I had the distinction of landing the first Thunderbolt in our squadron with full long range tanks. I was recalled from a mission and landed with no trouble at about 150mph on a 3 000 yard runway.

"I saw one of our aircraft come home with nine cylinders shot off by flak and another hit a palm tree on a low level run which only resulted in a dented wing."

Another squadron converting to the Thunderbolt was No 258 Squadron under the command of Squadron Leader Neil Cameron. His story is an excellent account of how Royal Air Force pilots reacted to the conversion to the Thunderbolt, their first experience of the phenomenon of compressibility and of the types of missions which the pilots carried out.

"The squadrons being re-equipped had either been on Hurricanes or the Bristol Blenheim and the Thunderbolt's performance was, of course, a degree different. Being a single-seat fighter-bomber the dual instruction had to be done on the blackboard with some hours in Harvard aircraft. I, personally, went straight from the Hurricane to the Thunderbolt without any difficulty and without instruction as did many of my pilots.

"The first aircraft were Thunderbolt Is with the old type latticed hoods, but being the third squadron to re-equip we received Thunderbolt IIs with the electrically operated bubble canopy. I had about two months to re-equip and train the squadron before flying back into Burma for operations. During training we had only one accident, which was a fatal one, and came about because an Australian

Early Thunderbolt Is of 134 Squadron during late 1944, when the unit was training on these aircraft in India. A group of pilots look up critically to assess a low level 'beat up' by a 'vic' of their unit's machines. At this stage the Thunderbolts do not carry the familiar white nose, wing and tail recognition bands, later applied to all such aircraft in SEAC.

sergeant-pilot tried to dive the Thunderbolt as fast as it could go. He discovered the implications of 'compressibility' but, unfortunately, did not live to tell the tale and pass the message on to others. However, it was pretty clear what had happened and the warning got about but it was interesting to note that this was our first experience of the shock waves which you could get into by diving the heavy Thunderbolt earthwards. Compressibility and all its hazards have now passed into history but it seems quite extraordinary that we knew so little about high speed aerodynamics towards the end of 1944.

"What it did prove to us was that the Thunderbolt could dive away from anything once it was headed on a downward path — a technique which was to prove useful later when we started operations against the Japanese.

"The training period of eight weeks was taken up with the art of dive bombing strafing with the .50 calibre machine guns, skip bombing, smoke laying and of course the numerous other manoeuvers required of a fighter-bomber. I moved the squadron to the outskirts of Madras for the dive bombing phase at an airfield called Arkonam. There was another Thunderbolt squadron on the base and we had two reasonable tarmac runways. I set up a bombing range between the runways so that we could carry out a vast number of practice bomb attacks which helped to hurry on the training programme. There were a few stray bombs, but no damage.

"Soon after I took the squadron up to Burma to an airfield called Cox's Bazaar. There were two other Thunderbolt squadrons there and we gradually built up the force to eight squadrons of 16 aircraft each. Our role was fighter-bomber and fighter activity and long-range escort missions in support of Liberator aircraft which were attacking the Japanese in the Rangoon area and southwards. Compared with Europe these raids were not enormous but on most of them there were at least 150 aircraft in the formation. Whilst doing these escort missions we flew with three long range tanks and there was usually some skirmishing with Japanese fighters over Rangoon itself and several of the airfield targets which were attacked. (Sqdn. Leader Cameron is credited with downing a Tony fighter over Rangoon on February 11th, 1945.) By then the Japanese were not engaging us in any great numbers and some of their tactics indicated that they knew little of the Thunderbolt's performance. Normally top cover for the bombers was flown by P-38 aircraft of the United States AAF whilst the Thunderbolts provided medium cover. The Japanese clearly did not realise the diving speed and stability of the Thunderbolt gun platform and, indeed, they failed to use their great advantage of maneuverability. We found it important to use the dive and climb tactics against the Zero, similar in a way to those used by the Me 109 against the Spitfire and Hurricane in the European theatre.

"In December 1944 we started to

Below: Burma workhorses, old and new. At dispersal sit the RAF's faithful Hurricane IIC fighter-bombers, most shrouded against dust. Past them taxi the first of their newly-arrived successors — Thunderbolt Is (P-47D 'razorbacks'), equipped with long-range tanks. It is September 1944.

Right: A line of RAF Thunderbolt Is are prepared for flight, now fully marked with white recognition bands, as three such aircraft, all fitted with long range drop tanks, thunder into the air.

Below right: Even before the first RAF Thunderbolt squadrons had got into action in September 1944, Mark IIs (P-47D-25s with 'bubble' cockpit canopies) were arriving in much greater numbers than the Mark Is. Here a dozen of these new fighters carrying the RS squadron code letters of 30 Squadron, fly a tight squadron formation.

receive our first supplies of napalm. It was a simple weapon system of long range tanks being filled with the new mixture and with a detonator applied to the tail. The tactics were to run in low over the targets, such as Japanese foxholes, jettison the tanks, which as a rule blew up in contact with the ground, and the usual napalm throw-forward and fire developed. We used napalm a lot and in hilly jungle country we were quite often asked to burn down a whole side of a hill so that the army could see the foxhole targets which otherwise had been covered by trees.

"The Thunderbolt also proved its great ability to take punishment. One of my pilots flew through his own bomb bursts by pulling out of his dive too late and, on his return to base, we found the base plate of one of his bombs lodged in the wing, but the aircraft was still flying though full of a great many holes!

"I moved my squadron with two others down to Ramree Island, off the Burma coast, for the assault on Rangoon. As it happened, though we carried out a great many attacks to soften up the Rangoon area the Japanese had, on the whole, pulled out before the assault craft went in.

"As the army continued to be successful we were employed largely on 'cab-rank' activities using four aircraft per squadron carrying two 1 000 pound bombs. We were called in to the target by the army teams — first bombing it and then carrying out strafing attacks. By the number of signals we received from the army it was clear that these attacks were very effective and the Japanese were discomfited to say the least!

"As regards an assessment of the Thunderbolt — all my crews became extremely fond of it and its operational performance. Certainly it was not a very manoeuvrable aircraft but by using its extraordinary diving speed with a subsequent pull up this was the type of tactic we taught for fighter to fighter activity. The bulk of our work, however, was in strafing and bombing targets in support of the army and also in long range escorts. I always found the aircraft was extremely stable and easy to fly on a long sortie. The most uncomfortable aspect was sitting on a dinghy pack for four to five hours. It was also an excellent aircraft for formation flying with great control in all axes. I think that if we had run into large numbers of high performance Japanese fighters we might have been in some trouble but generally speaking operating at 30 000 feet and above we were well above

their top ceiling and therefore usually had a height advantage."

Squadron Leader Cameron went on to pursue a career in the Royal Air Force and is now Air Chief Marshal Sir Neil Cameron, GCB, CBE, DSO, DFC, RAF and Chief of Air Staff.

All of the RAF pilots who flew the Thunderbolt in Burma agree that the 'cab-rank' missions did a great deal of damage to the Japanese, both physically and mentally. Arthur B. Skidmore who flew with No 5 Squadron stated: "The degree of accuracy obtained in dive bombing reached such a level that attacks on targets within 100 yards of our own troops were not uncommon."

However, his squadron did encounter some difficulty during the period in which they were flying these type of missions.

"We suffered unexplained casualties from mid-air explosions occuring at the point of highest 'G' loading on pull-out from the dive. It was rectified by changing fuel management in a manner that reduced the amount remaining in the main tank during the attack. A simple fix, but one that took time and caused some morale problems."

While their story is largely unsung, the Thunderbolts of the Royal Air Force turned in a very creditable record and inflicted untold damage upon the Japanese in Burma up to the very end of the war.

Left: Alongside the squadron's long range fuel tank dump, Thunderbolt IIs of 30 Squadron are prepared for a sortie by their ground crews.

Below left: 134 Squadron began operations over Burma in December 1944, just in time to deliver this Christmas gift! 'Jungle Queen' is a Mark II Thunderbolt.

Below: One of the first two units to take the Thunderbolt into action with the RAF in Burma was 261 Squadron, a unit with a chequered and varied past. This 250lb bomb-carrying Mark II is serialled KJ225, and was flown by F/Sgt Rowley.

Bottom: By 1945 the need for camouflage on fighter aircraft had diminished, and many of the later Thunderbolt IIs to be delivered retained the natural metal finish common to their USAAF counterparts at this time. The white recognition markings were not practical in such cases, and were replaced by black or 'roundel blue' paint. KL849 of 261 Squadron is being flown by the commanding officer, Sqn Ldr R. H. Fletcher.

Above: As the war in Burma drew to a close, a number of the Thunderbolt squadrons which had given such good service, were re-numbered. In the foreground, carrying the new codes AW, are camouflaged aircraft of 146 Squadron, which had now become 42 Squadron (previously a Hurricane unit, now disbanded). To the rear, coded NV, are aircraft of another of the original Thunderbolt squadrons, No79, which retained its own number.

Centre right: Ex-146 Squadron, now 42 Squadron, an early Thunderbolt II (KJ358) is seen here in flight over Southern Burma in late Summer 1945.

Bottom right: A squadron which saw sustained operations with the Thunderbolt, both as a fighter-bomber and as a bomber escort unit, was 258 Squadron. One of this unit's Thunderbolt IIs (KL314) is seen here just after the end of the war, after moving from Burma to Malaya's Kuala Lumpur airfield.

140

Above: A 'silver' Thunderbolt of 42 Squadron at Meiktila, Burma, in 1945. This aircraft, which was flown by Sqn Ldr 'Bill' Soutters, had its recognition bands painted in 'roundel blue'.

Centre right: Last RAF unit to receive the Thunderbolt was 60 Squadron, which re-equipped in June 1945. Too late to use these aircraft operationally in Burma, the squadron was to undertake some strikes against Indonesian guerrillas in Java on behalf of the Dutch in November 1945.

Bottom right: Hallmark of a great fighter squadron. In July 1945, 81 Squadron, which had flown Spitfires in Burma with great distinction, was disbanded. Its squadron number, letters (FL) and 'Ace of Spades' insignia, were all transferred to 123 Squadron, which had been operating Thunderbolts in the fighter-bomber role in Burma since the previous December. Like 60 Squadron, this unit was to see further brief action in Java in November 1945.

Nose Art

The nose of a 373rd Fighter Group P-47.

The youthful spirit of the fighter pilots of World War II was exemplified by the colourful nose art carried on their Thunderbolts. The quality varied to great degrees for some units possessed the talents of some very fine artists and some did not. Regardless, most all seemed to come up with an interesting variety of subjects; the greatest by far being the most important attraction to a pilot in his early 20s — girls. (Above) 373rd Fighter Group. (Right) 56th Fighter Group (Below) 366th Fighter Group. (Far right) 366th Fighter Group. (Below right) 365th Fighter Group.

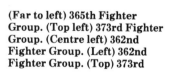

(Far to left) 365th Fighter Group. (Top left) 373rd Fighter Group. (Centre left) 362nd Fighter Group. (Left) 362nd Fighter Group. (Top) 373rd Fighter Group. (Above) 354th Fighter Group. (Above right) 373rd Fighter Group. (Below) 4th Fighter Group. (Right) 4th Fighter Group.

Other Places

Right: P-47D-21-RE sits poised on Chinese airfield. Most Chinese airfields were made of crushed rock, spread and rolled down by the natives.

Below: P-47-Ds of 92nd Fighter Squadron are made ready for a long-range mission from their Chinese base. All are fully loaded with wing and belly fuel tanks.

In the course of World War II the Thunderbolt saw extensive service in the China-Burma-India Theatre of operations with the United States Army Air Force and the Royal Air Force. Over 800 P-47-Ds were allocated to the Royal Air Force and most of them were stationed in Southeast Asia. Used primarily in support of the British 14th Army these aircraft performed yeoman duty in Burma, mostly on dive bombing and strafing missions. The CBI Thunderbolts also attacked enemy airfields and did some escort work especially with the

fleets of cargo-carrying aircraft which dropped supplies to forward areas.

The United States had several units operating P-47s in the theatre in 1944. The 80th Fighter Group received its Thunderbolts in the spring of 1944 and spent a great deal of its time escorting C-46 and C-47 flying 'The Hump' between India and China.

Some of the types of missions flown by the 80th Group are described by F. Doug Parsons: "We flew a lot of bombing and strafing missions against airfields railroads, bridges and enemy troop

movements. We also flew a lot of ground support missions in Northern Burma often strafing Japanese forces right in the front lines.

"Several times we intercepted movements of Japanese cavalry units. On one occasion a flight of four P-47s sighted a troop of enemy cavalry on a road. The Japanese immediately dismounted and took cover in high elephant grass. I split the flight up, two planes to go after the horses and two after the troops. In a short while we had pretty well annihilated both components.

"On another occasion we caught Japanese cavalry moving down a river on ferry boats. As we made our first pass low over the boat, most of the troops jumped overboard. We were still each carrying two 500 pound bombs which we proceeded to drop in the water. What this didn't take care of we finished off by strafing.

"One significant strafing mission I took part in was directed at the Japanese airfield at Lashio. This was quite a distance from our base at Myitkyina so we took off before dawn loaded with wing tanks. We flew at relatively high altitude on the way down until we were quite close then we dropped our wing tanks and descended to the deck.

"As we approached the airfield we pull-

ed up to 250-300 feet and spaced ourselves out about a half a block apart in line abreast for the strafing run. As a rule we only made one pass when strafing for this alerted the enemy's ground defences and a subsequent run was too risky.

"On this particular attack my wingman flew right through a Japanese aircraft hangar, in one side and out the other. At first I thought he must be horsing around, but evidently he was hit by the intense machine-gun fire we encountered as we went across the field, for upon emerging from the hangar his P-47 bellied in on the edge of the field.

"We made several other passes to suppress the ground defence and give him a chance to make a break for it should he have survived the landing. We saw no activity around the Thunderbolt, however, so we climbed up and headed for home."

The 33rd and the 81st Fighter Groups were taken out of the Mediterranean theatre and sent to India to become Thunderbolt units. Originally they had been destined to become escort fighters for the B-29s operating out of China, but this goal was never achieved. The 33rd Group carried out its operations primarily over Burma while the 81st saw considerable service in China.

Above left: Aligned at their base in Asanol, India, are P-47-Ds of the 1st Air Commando Group. This unit flew ground support in Burma and also escorted bombers to Rangoon.

Left: Zebra striped Thunderbolt 'Pitt's Pott' flown by Captain Pitts of 1 ACG. Note directional finding loop antenna. The long distances involved in operations in this theatre made these navigational aids a must.

Above: Chinese guards provide a toothy grin while mechanic changes spark plugs on an 81st FG Thunderbolt.

Top: This 81st Fighter Group P-47 made it home to a belly landing after taking extensive damage from enemy ground fire.

Above: Shiny new P-47D-30 in front of Chinese hangar at Hsian in Northwest China.

Right: 81st Fighter Group Thunderbolt comes in over the rocky end barrier of runway 21 at its Chinese airfield.

Other Models

During the course of the war several models of the P-47 were produced but were never put into production. The first of these was the XP-47-E which featured a pressurised cabin. This model got no further than the protytpe stage.

Then came the XP-47-F which utilised a laminar flow wing. This wing featured low drag characteristics, but the advantages gained were not worth putting it into production. The prototype aircraft went to Wright Field for testing and it flew a number of experimental flights before crashing in October 1943.

Two P-47-D s were taken from the production line in late 1943 as test beds for the Chrysler 16-cylinder, inverted-vee, liquid cooled engine. This engine had teething troubles for many months, however, and the war was almost over before the XP-47-H, as the in-line engined version of the aircraft was designated, ever took to the air.

The XP-47-J was a lightweight version of the Thunderbolt which utilized the R-2800-57 'C' series engine, with maximum rating of 2 800 horse power. The airframe

was cleaned up by removing the wing pylons and all external stores. Only six guns were fitted and ammunition load was cut. The XP-47-J first flew in the summer of 1944 and it reached the 500mph mark. Further testing was not quite as successful, however, and the retooling that would have been necessary to put the aircraft into production was never begun.

After World War II the P-47 was largely withdrawn from the active rolls of the US Army Air Forces, but a number were relegated to Air National Guard units. Many found their way to South American countries and the Chinese Nationalists flew them for some years.

Today only a handful exist. The most prominent of these aircraft are the six still flying in service with the 'Confederate Air Force' located at Harlingen, Texas, and one flying as a special project of the Puerto Rican Air National Guard.

Above: P-47-N beautifully restored by members of Puerto Rican Air National Guard. World War II markings used are those of the 345 Fighter Squadron, 350th Fighter Group, 12th Air Force. This aircraft was flown all the way, from Puerto Rica to California for the 1973 Thunderbolt Pilots' Reunion.

Left: Six ex-Peruvian AF P-47-Ns in formation over Harlingen, Texas. Confederate Air Force has restored and finished them in the markings of outstanding World War II aces and fighter groups.

3/4 REAR VIEW (XP-47F) 6-25-42

Above: Photo made during the construction of the one and only P-47-F. This aircraft had a laminar flow wing but this did not improve performance enough for the model to be put into production.

Centre left: The light-weight P-47-J had the R-2800-57 'C' engine which had a maximum horsepower rating of 2,800. Its speed exceeded 500 miles per hour but it was not put into production.

Bottom left: The in-line liquid cooled engine powered P-47-H. This model with the Chrysler built engine developed 2,500 hp, but experienced many teething problems.

157

Top left: Under test. Though never employed by the RAF in Europe, the Thunderbolt was tested in the United Kingdom, and here two of these fighters (the nearest HD267) are seen in standard Fighter Command camouflage and markings.

Centre left: While not equipping any operational RAF squadrons in the Mediterranean area, a substantial number of Thunderbolts were issued to 73 Operational Training Unit at Fayid, Egypt. Here these were painted with the unit's unusual 'Ace of Spades-with-Death's Head' marking on their noses. This makes interesting comparison with the insignia applied by 81 Squadron.

Left: His cockpit hood still open, a pilot climbs away after take-off in a 73 OTU Thunderbolt II.

Above: By early 1945 seven Groupes of P-47Ds were operational with the Armeé de l'Air in Europe, flying tactical fighter-bomber missions in support of the Allied forces facing the Siegfried Line defences on the Franco-German frontier. These aircraft, taxiing through the snow of the hard 1944/45 winter, each carry a pair of 250lb bombs beneath the wings.

Centre right: A rare bird. Following the Allied occupation of French North Africa, the Armeé de l'Air once more became a substantial fighting force in the Allied armoury. One of the main types supplied during 1944 was the P-47D, but few 'razorbacks' reached the French. Ex-USAAF 42-26157, which has completed a substantial number of operational sorties with its new owners, is seen here on Beja airfield, Tunisia, in September 1944. It carries the 'Greyhound' emblem of 4 Escadrille, Groupe de Chasse II/3 'Dauphine', beneath the cockpit.

Bottom right: P-47Ds remained in service with the Armeé de l'Air long after the end of World War II, subsequently seeing further action against the FLN guerrillas in Algeria during the fifties. Here a natural metal French P-47D, carrying black and white stripes round its rear fuselage, climbs into the sky.

159

Photo Credits